Contextual Theology

The Drama of Our Times

Paul Duane Matheny

Ⓒ

James Clarke & Co

James Clarke & Co
P.O. Box 60
Cambridge
CB1 2NT
United Kingdom

www.jamesclarke.co
publishing@jamesclarke.co

ISBN: 978 0 227 68012 4

British Library Cataloguing in Publication Data
A record is available from the British Library

First Published by James Clarke & Co, 2012

Copyright © Paul Duane Matheny, 2011

Published by arrangement
with Pickwick Publications

Contents

Preface

THE RECOMMENDATION TO USE contextual methods in theology is not new. As the global South began to recover from the blanket domination of the developed nations after World War II, theological educators assessed the situation and proposed new models of theological formation. Soon the expectation arose that theological education should be contextual. While there is some confusion about what this means, there is a consensus that the core curriculum for theological study in the global South should be contextual. This expectation is growing and not waning as the decades go by.

The situation is once again changing. As a new post-colonial reality took form, the failure to acknowledge the contextual nature of theology became acute. The advocacy of a link between Western culture and theology was discovered to be a danger weakening the integrity of communities of faith. Colonialism had led to ethnic humiliation and racist ideologies embedded in the sense of local identity. The distrust of local culture was and continues to be bound up with power struggles, social hierarchies, and social policing.

Some leaders believed that Western scholarship did not understand or address these issues and tended to ignore or marginalize the problems that they raised. The Western churches had their own problems and challenges. One has only to think of the current debate over homosexuality in the West as evidence for the current distrust that is evident around the world.

In addition Western missionaries and ideas are often experienced as foreign and unacceptably alien. The old question of cultural mediation has risen in a new context with new challenges. As modernization has raced in nations like India and China, the turn toward contextualization has taken on a new urgency. The struggles of the powerless have been fundamentally transformed and have consequently set the stage for new ecclesial realities. Around the globe these transformations have engendered new spiritualities and a hunger for religious experience. The extraordinary growth of charismatic movements has altered the religious landscape so that it is no longer familiar. This lack of familiarity makes church leaders and theologians nervous. It is easier to react than respond.

Theologians today are facing a significantly different world than that of the 60s and 70s when the proposal to contextualize theological education was first made. A "new Christianity" has arisen as the epicenter of Christianity has moved away from the West and to the global South. We are just now beginning to realize the differences and what they may mean. Contextual theologies in the 60s and 70s became identified with the liberation theologies of Latin America and colluded often with the growth of nationalism in the Third World. These theologies could become ideologically laden and/or ethnic expressions. They are being re-configured and new theological and ecclesial paths are being forged. Current transformations are calling for the use contextualizing methods. Something new is happening and the need for contextualizing methods is apparent.

We can no longer simply repeat the traditional answers to old questions; we need to respond to the questions that are rising as the problem of what it means to be Christian in this new situation is being faced. As the profundity of the gospel is experienced in new contexts, the implications of this message for Christian living are being illumined. We are seeing this happening in new approaches to biblical and theological interpretation. It is becoming clearer that theology is not the work of an individual, but of the praxis and cultural mediation of concrete communities of faith. As Christians are facing new challenges of Christian living they are regrouping Christian traditions and wisdom for new purposes. The new search for understanding by the faithful around the globe can become a way to protect the "new Christianity" from the lure of illusion and preserve the desire for truth. Contextual theology's role in making this happen is essential. Perhaps it can restore theology to its proper role to invite all to live according to the purposes of God. Contextual theology can remind us of the dangers of ignoring God in the face of the threat to life that our new situation entails. It can cement for us the connection between our work in the local church and the purposes of God for all of creation. It reminds us that our mission is part of God's mission for the whole world.

Introduction

Hopes that the future of theology lies among the new "contextual" theologies of the "new Christianity" abound. Could these theologies replace the theologies of the Atlantic cultures with their roots in ancient theology and doctrine? For some this hope has given carte blanche to any theology from the global South that calls into question traditional "Western" theology. For others the emergence of non-Western Christian thinking is insignificant for it seems to have little to add to the theological debate. I believe these claims to be misleading and disingenuous. The theologies of the "new Christianity" cannot be easily pigeonholed in anti-traditional garb, nor are they irrelevant for scholarship. Many theologians from the Third World, for example, are very traditional in their stances. They are struggling to provide theological guidelines for their churches. Our prejudices get the best of us when we picture the theologians of these lands as newly evangelized, for example. This is anything but the case; Latin American and Filipino churches, for example, are centuries old. Imagining their theologians to be new to the faith is evidence of our failure to come to terms with the new reality of the strength of non-Western Christianity.

We will see that what is new about these theologies is that they are holding up the importance of contextual methods in approaching the Christian life and faith. These theologies are new in the willingness to connect the proclamation of the gospel and the living of the Christian faith to the historical, socio-cultural, political and cultural realities of the people who attempt to be Christian in lands of the global South and East.[1] Their faith in Jesus Christ has led them to seek culturally and socially au-

1. A term that refers to global regions that are not "Western" is difficult to find. I will use the phrases "the global South" and the "new Christianity" to refer to the "non-Western" churches that have been established through the mission work of the Atlantic churches—the European and American churches from the continent, the USA, and Canada. Both terms are unsatisfactory in that they are neither all new nor all found in the southern hemisphere. The blurring of the boundaries is part of the discussion being addressed here.

thentic ways to contribute to the building up of the common faith shared by Christians everywhere and in all ages.

The insights of non-Western contextual theologies are to inform more than just their own communities. When insights about the process of theological reflection arise in any context they are commensurable and helpful across cultures. While this is a controversial point, there is a consensus that commensurability is a necessary characteristic of the theological processes of Christian faith communities. This is the common experience of Christian theologies around the globe. Two things that have been learned during the past several decades after contextual theology came on the stage are that Christology is vital and that the problem of the liberation of the oppressed and marginalized is unavoidable, given the depth of human poverty and suffering throughout the world. These insights belong now to the entire Christian tradition, exactly because of the development of contextual theology as part of the theological process of churches, both "new" and "established" worldwide.

The purpose of this book is to examine the changes in our understanding of theological processes in the life of the Christian churches due to the introduction of contextual methods. The examination will lead us to new insights into the nature of theological and ethical work of Christian communities. I will suggest strategies for enriching Christian theology arising from these insights. This introduction has initiated a change in the approach to the role of theological reflection for Christians that is of historic significance. Both scholars and church leaders are doing theology in new ways. They are driven by the conviction that contextual methods make it possible for theology to do what it is supposed to do. Throughout the Third World, for example, the expectation is widespread that the curriculum and theological formation programs of denominations, seminaries, and theological schools must be "contextual". Accordingly, theological education should never lose sight of the problems and realities of the churches and people that they serve. This is much easier expected than realized. There is much to improve, but the hope is authentic. Frequently, faculty and students complain that the expectation is stated but not instituted. The means and the understanding necessary to implement the expectation are not at hand. This has led, on the one hand, to the adoption of theologies that have little to do with contextual methods and, on the other hand, to the uncritical use of "Western" textbooks and modes of thinking. The failure to connect with the churches of the "new Christianity" has led to works of non-Western scholars being unavailable in their own countries, but available in the West, and to theological developments in the Third World and the West that are not discussed or even shared with other Christians. Among Western theologians this lack of clarity has led to uncritical responses to Third World theology and philosophy, where an attitude of tolerant disinterest and voyeuristic curiosity abound. A goal of this book is to promote a deeper and more global understanding of the promise of contextual methods in theology for theological educators worldwide. My reflections are aimed at retrieving the significance of the use of contextual methods for Christian mission and theology, and thereby to foster ecumenical vision among Christian communities everywhere.

The neologisms, contextual theology and contextual method, are a product of the theological ferment during the period after WWII and the founding of the World Council of Churches. The concepts appeared in theological literature in early forms as the discussion about the theology of the "emerging" churches flared. In 1945 the first Henry W. Luce Professor of World Christianity at Union Theological Seminary in New York, the Chinese scholar Francis Cho-Min Wei, argued that Christianity must find an Asian cultural foundation whereby it could foster the mutual enrichment of Christians and cultures throughout the globe. He prophesied that the future depended upon the willingness of every culture and expression of the Christian faith to contribute to the dawning of a global Christian fellowship.[2] Soon afterward, Henry Paul Van Dusen proclaimed that "to an age destined to survive, or to expire, as 'one world,' we bring a world church." Van Dusen believed that world Christianity had become a world reality.[3] These insights were to be re-confirmed repeatedly in the decades ahead, with layers of new perspectives, promises, disappointments, and transformations.

The sense that something was dawning had sparked enthusiasm for the ecumenical movement and for theological education. In 1957 the Rockefeller Foundation established a fund for "contextualizing the gospel." In the 60s and 70s new ideas were floated that responded to the needs of newly post-colonial nations. In the 60s the scholars, Paul Lehmann and Daniel Van Allem, worked out a theological framework for contextual theology. In the 70s, Shoki Coe and the staff of the Theological Education

2. Wei, *The Spirit of Chinese Culture*, 28.

3. Van Dusen, *World Christianity*, 248ff.

Fund of the World Council of Churches, including James Burtness and Aharon Sapsezian, proposed using contextual methods in order to reform the theological education of the churches recovering from colonialism and world war.

One of the most influential developments of the new interest in contextual methods in theology was the birth in 1976 of the Ecumenical Association of Third World Theologians or EATWOT. It was organized as a means to encourage Third World theologians. The first meeting occurred in Dar-es-Salaam, Tanzania and the focus was on the "emergent gospel." The struggle continues today. One of the more recent meetings occurred in Manila, Philippines in 1996 where they focused on the challenge of a just world order for Christian theology. Kofi Appiah-Kubi speaking at the Pan-African Conference of Third World Theologians held in Ghana in December of 1977 summarized the upshot of these new developments for theologians. He declared, "African theologians" are trying to "find a theology that speaks to our people where we are, to enable us to answer the critical question of our Lord Jesus Christ: 'Who do you (African Christians) say that I am?'"[4]

Another organization that arose in response to the new interest in contextual theology is the Association of Theological Education in South East Asia. It was to this organization that Karl Barth wrote his final pastoral letter for *The South East Asia Journal of Theology*, Autumn 1969, encouraging them to "say that which you have to say as Christians for God's sake, responsibly and concretely with your own words and thoughts, concepts and ways! The more responsibly and concretely, the better, the more Christian!"[5] Later in 1972 this organization formulated a Critical Asian Principle with the intent to transform theological education and mission in South East Asia according to "contextual" principles.[6]

---

4. Appiah-Kubi and Torres, eds. *African Theology en Route*, viii.

5. Karl Barth, "Barth's Last Pastoral Letter," v.

6. The *Critical Asian Principle* was adopted by the ATSEA to provide the basic guidelines for doctoral research conducted by their graduate school, the South East Asia Graduate School of Theology (SEAGST). It was proposed first in an article written for ATSEA by Ermito Nacpil in 1972 and then in the assembly of the Senate of SEAGST. Theology was to be conducted in terms of a frame of reference circumscribed by situational, hermeneutical, missiological, and educational areas of concern. These areas correspond to culture, scripture, tradition, experience, and reason serving as sources for theological work in the process of "contextualization," however it is perceived. See *Minutes of the Senate of SEAGST*, Bangkok, February 1972 and *Minutes of the Senate of*

In addition to the theologies from scholars from the global South, theologians from Atlantic nations, such as Lesslie Newbigin, James Cone, Douglas John Hall, and Jürgen Moltmann, have taken contextual methods seriously in their work. The theory of contextual methods is now part of theological study throughout the globe. It is becoming clear that contextual theology is necessary for helpful awareness of our era's reality, characterized by suffering, modernity, and political, philosophical, and economic pluralism. Mission, evangelism, and scholarship need to tackle the questions of context, or those of the quotidian breadth of everyday experience. The thin and abstract theologian of the past needs to be replaced with depth and concreteness in order to face the challenges of our global Christianity and the needs of local church communities rooted in their culture and their struggles.

The trenchant point of contextual theology is that theologians and pastors should take the lives of people seriously. It provides us with a means to measure the quality of our theology according to this expectation. Good theology keeps the church in touch with reality. It forces the church to see the world of its mission, work and proclamation. Through the use of contextual methods, theologians, pastors, and lay people can learn to speak each other's languages. In order to ensure that a healthy theology takes place, reality must be faced as we participate in the *missio Dei*. Contextual theology is the part of the theological process that intends to do just that. Many believe that the way we do theology has been changed forever by the recovery of the contextual. It is time to examine with rigor and faithfulness the drama that is unfolding.

SEAGST, 1972, GS7209. According to such an understanding, the task of theology and the mission of the church in a particular context were never to be separated.

1

The Church Looks to the Future

The Encouragement of Contextual Methods in Theology?

THE TURNING POINTS OF CHRISTIAN MISSION
TRIGGER CONTEXTUAL THEOLOGY

THE HISTORY OF CHRISTIANITY has exhibited surprising and dramatic turning points during the last century. A century ago, commentators declared that the twentieth century would be the most hopeful and promising of any period in history. William Temple, the Archbishop of Canterbury, declared early in the century at his installation as Archbishop of Canterbury that Christianity was a worldwide reality.[1] He and others speculated about this new turn of events and prophesied great and exciting changes. At the beginning of the century John Mott wrote a classic of the times. The title says it in a nutshell: *The Evangelization of the World in this Generation.*[2] Remarkably, during the first half of the century and in spite of the changing fortunes of colonialism, conservative and liberal theologies, and scientific culture, the hope for a global Christianity continued to rise. Colonialism yielded to anti-imperialist nationalism; optimistic philosophy based upon logic and science was humbled by post-modern rejection of foundational thinking in any form; mission that espoused Western values and cultural traditions yielded to evangelism that is rooted in the struggles of indigenous peoples. Yet the hope for a global Christianity seems to be ever-present in spite of these changes and perhaps due to the fact of the success of the mission efforts. Barriers

---

1. Temple, *The Church Looks Forward*, 2–4.

2. Mott, *The Evangelization of the World.* Enthusiasm for world evangelism and mission continued right up to the beginning of WWII. See Mott, ed. *Evangelism for the World Today.*

attempting to block the growth of mission efforts seemed to be thrown up at every point during the last century up until the first decades of the twenty-first century. The turn to contextual methods in theology is part of the effort to fulfill that hope.

The cultural and social trauma of the twentieth century has taken a toll on mission theology and practice. At the beginning of the twentieth century, the mood of Western Christianity was high. Consciously or unconsciously enthused by the excitement of scientific progress and Western colonial influence, Christian leaders believed as well in Christian advancement. This enthusiasm mirrored and colluded with the confidence in moral and scientific progress. It was to be a Christian century—thus the name of the popular journal *The Christian Century* published since the beginning of twentieth century in conjunction with the founding of COCU and the Divinity School of the University of Chicago.[3] Piety and progress were wedded together by a politics of intervention and dominance. Fundamentalism and liberal theology competed for the scientific worldview and confessional theology arose to counteract the dark-side of secularism and science. Racism, which had been such a comfortable partner for colonialism, had bitten the hand that gave it birth, and began catalyzing ethnic warfare throughout the world.[4] I am sure that neither William Temple nor John Mott could have imagined what became of world Christianity and the world, if they had been given the opportunity to look back at the century from the promontory of the first decade of the twenty-first century.

Rudyard Kipling called upon Americans at the beginning of the twentieth century to take up the "white man's burden" and convert

---

3. Peter Ainslie III's address to the 1910 International Convention of the Christian Church (Disciples of Christ) "Our Fellowship and the Task," the lecture that inaugurated the Council on Christian Union (COCU), argued that indifference to the worldwide ecumenical unity of the Christian churches is a mark of "grave disloyalty to Christ." See Ainslie III, *Toward Christian Unity*. In 1900, the editor of a small Christian magazine published in Des Moines, Iowa proposed to rename the magazine *Christian Century* in response to the great optimism at the beginning of the twentieth century that "genuine Christian faith could live in mutual harmony with the modern developments in science, technology, immigration, communication, and culture that were already under way." In conjunction with this new emphasis, the Century's offices moved to Chicago. From this inauspicious beginning the magazine became a leading voice for liberal Christianity and mainstream Protestantism. The Divinity School was founded in the same liberal spirit.

4. Ferguson, *War of the World*.

the world to "progress" and "civilization".[5] Echoing Protestant leaders around the country, President William McKinley spoke of the success of American missions as a "triumph of civilization."[6] The Christian West was experiencing a fever for evangelism, motivated by faith and simultaneously stimulated by the arrogance of cultural chauvinism. A marriage of aggression with religious and moral conviction worked itself out in the "fields" of mission work, in ways that diminished the lives of the very people they sought to serve. At the height of this enthusiasm mission studies was an integral part of the curriculum of seminaries and theological schools throughout the West. Today, as a response to this chauvinism, it has been marginalized.

At the beginning of the twenty-first century the mood is very different. Mission studies is a peripheral subject in most seminaries and theological schools, sometimes led by professors who are opposed to the "sending of missionaries" to foreign countries. In addition the mainstream churches that fired the earlier movement have lost their grit and their ground. They lost ground among the peoples of the West and are losing members in what seems to be a free fall with no end in sight. They cling to their heritages with little awareness of the global changes that ebb around them, lapping at their social and cultural boundaries and eroding their futures.[7]

Today the "evangelizing nations" are weak evangelists at best, while the epicenter of Christianity is migrating to the South settling among the homes of the peoples who were once identified by church leaders from the West as "mission fields." Secularism in the West has led many to become "neo-pagans" and uncommitted.[8] While the millions who live

---

5. Kipling, "To Take Up the White Man's Burden."

6. Anderson, "American Protestants in Pursuit of Mission," 384. An example of a Protestant leader who saw the conquest of the Philippines by the United States in providential terms is Rev. John Henry Barrows, President of Oberlin College. Cf. "The Christian Conquest of Asia," the Morse Lectures delivered at Union Theological Seminary of New York City in late 1898, published as Barrows, *The Christian Conquest of Asia*, xi, 238, 248. He wrote, ". . . wherever on pagan shores the voice of the American missionary and teacher is heard, there is fulfilled the manifest destiny of the Christian Republic." This theme is discussed in Anderson, "Providence and Politics," 279ff.

7. Hanciles, "Birth and Bankruptcy," 84ff.

8. Taylor, *A Secular Age*, 612–13, 770–73. Here Charles Taylor wrote, "Much of our deep past cannot simply be laid aside, not just because of our "weakness," but because there is something genuinely important and valuable in it. Recognizing this fact, in our present culture, usually means being anti-Christian, embracing some of the values of

in Europe and America and call themselves Christian live out their faith uninformed about the scriptures, and dissuaded of Christian ethical and doctrinal expectations and traditions of Christian convictions. Both Christianity's critics and adherents are little concerned with the depth of Christian faith and the integrity of its beliefs. Such critics of religion as Richard Dawkins can make up his own dream Christianity without even well educated intellectuals knowing the difference. In the Third World, in contrast, Christians and non-Christians alike are often eager to learn more about Christian beliefs. Chinese scholars, Africans from indigenous tribes, and former Soviet atheists are but a few examples of persons hoping for the retrieval of commitment to the Christian faith and its promulgation. The non-Western world is now the home of the great majority of Christians, while committed Christians in Europe are few and far between.

This points to the queer significance of the legacy of Christendom and of the escalating importance of the migration of Christianity into new cultural and social domains. Christendom in its many forms is now a part of history and participation in Christendom no longer plays a role as a pre-requisite and privilege for Christian identity. The question facing Christian leaders and theologians today is whether we will be effective in uncovering and using resources that will ensure a healthy future for Christian faith. One ecumenical answer advocates the retrieval of insight from pre-Constantinian Christianity to help resource the formation of the new Christianity emerging in the global South. The early church not only practiced a vigorous unity with diversity, it was a marked by a strong social and cultural identity that was not integrated with the civic culture of empire. The substance of the witness of the early church has been a source for inspiration in both the Reformation traditions and Catholic practices. The Christianity of the New Testament was blended with that of Christendom. Søren Kierkegaard and John Howard Yoder are two influential thinkers who have warned us about our failure to take seriously the Christianity of the New Testament.[9]

Prevalent throughout the globe is the answer that arose with the awareness of the reality of global Christianity. The response to the reality has been a broad affirmation of the necessity for contextual methods in

"paganism," or "polytheism." It is worthwhile to follow Taylor's suggestion to study the first volume of Peter Gay's *The Enlightenment*.

9. Kierkegaard, *Attack upon Christendom*.

doing theology, for models of theological education, and in contemporary understandings of mission and evangelism. In each case the initiative to implement a contextual response to this new awareness was
led by ecumenical and missional movements, Protestant, Catholic, and
evangelical.

During the centuries of Christendom, Western Christianity was too
often a religion without mission and when it did engage in mission it
did not hesitate to use coercion.[10] Christendom took a variety of forms,
as a consequence of a synergetic relationship of mutual benefit between
political, cultural, and social order; but it always took a form that left no
question about the Christian identity of their civilization. The development of this identity was marked by greater complexity and institutional
coalescence. In spite of the penetration of criticism, the contemporary
church in the West and perhaps as well in the new Christianity of the
global South is still living within the Christendom framework. Protestant
and Catholic churches are extensions of the Christendom form. Debates
in Europe and the USA continue to rage over the role of Christianity in
public life. Should Christianity remain a state religion? Should we allow
or even enforce prayer in school?

While providing a sturdy future for Christianity that even today
is hard to shake off, Christendom relied upon a huge distortion of the
relation of the nature of the church and mission. It is only recently that
the vital place of mission in the origin of Christian theology has been
recalled to the church's attention. Martin Kähler working as an historian
noted, "mission was the mother of earliest Christian theology."[11] For
the early church mission provided the context for Christian theology.
Mission was not a tool with imperialist goals that could be described as a
form of conquest. It provided the womb that gave birth, form, and shape
to theological thought.[12] Mission made theology possible and theology
participated in the vitality of mission.

10. Hanciles, *Beyond Christendom*, 90ff., 157ff. Expansion of "Christian" territory and
the creation of mission fields were intertwined with the Western missionary movement
after the Reformation and remained inseparable until the beginning of the twentieth
century and the end of colonialism. A re-thinking was compelled. Christian commitment was often conceived as the moral side of the world order, which was responsible
for its strength and provided a moral justification for the domination of colonialism.

11. Kähler, *Schriften zur Christologie und Mission.*

12. Volf and Bass, eds. *Practicing Theology.* In this valuable book the relationship of
theology to the birth, formation, and role of theological work is discussed in a variety

The result of Christendom's neglect of the relation of the nature of the church and mission was the separation of the church and God's mission, the *missio Dei*. The medieval church struggled over the form it should take. The problem that dominated their struggle was not the nature of God's mission, but the order of a Christian political and religious life. From the ninth century on, the debate centered on the three orders and the power of monks, kings, knights, merchants, and bishops.[13] The problem faced was that of vocation for members of a Christian society. How could a knight or a merchant be a Christian, if their way of life contradicted biblical and traditional teachings? Who had greater power in spiritual and secular matters, the abbot or the bishop? Was a king a sacred ruler, under the counsel of the pope, bishops, or abbots? In the end the question that plagued until this day, was the character of vocation.

When mission happened it was something carried on, if at all, by agencies and directed toward non-believers in foreign lands. A pattern of "us" (the Christians) and "them" (non-Christians) developed within the social imaginary of Western culture. The agencies coordinated missionaries with vocations recognizable by the structures of the church and the political order as coincident with and dovetailed to the growth and stability of Christendom—whose growth was vital for both. Ecclesiology focused on the role the church played in preserving order and proper doctrine in the social imaginary of everyone living within its domains.[14] Mission was no longer understood as the work of God among the peoples of the world, but as the expansion of ecclesial domain and rule.

Ecclesiology lost its verve and urgency. The church was no longer a missionary church, which witnessed and forms disciples. Today the hope to recover this verve has motivated new approaches to ecclesiology.

---

of ways with varying convictions. The conviction that theological reflection and work depends on the meaning of Christian practices runs throughout the text. Yet, the role of mission in making Christian living possible at all and therefore of providing a space for theological thinking at all is missing from the discussion.

13. Duby, *The Three Orders*.

14. Minear, *Images of the Church*. A very helpful contribution to the discussion concerning ecumenical and contextual theology is Paul Lehmann's essay "On Doing Theology: A Contextual Possibility," in *Prospect for Theology*, 117–36. This fine essay was written in support of the ecumenical movement's proposal to do theology using contextual methods. Consistently in the early stages of the turn to contextual and ecumenical theology, the proponents were confessional theologians and not theological pluralists. Theological pluralists were not supportive, given their desire to promote a universal philosophy of religion rather than a concrete theology of peoples of faith.

Scholars are returning to the biblical resources. A few words aside here will help illustrate this point. Stanley Skreslet's recent book, *Picturing Christian Witness*, provides resources for theological reflection that help us to recover the energy and vitality of an ecclesiology where the church is not interwoven with the interests of Christendom. He proposes that our task is to retrieve what it means to be the church from biblical traditions and stories. To do this we need to identify the work of a missionary church according to a biblical imaginary.[15] The images of mission he discovers in the Bible are not acts performed by agents with a particular vocation in a Christian society, but events necessary for the integrity and spirituality of the life of the church. For there to be mission the church needs to "announce the Good News," "share Christ" with friends, "interpret the gospel," "shepherd" as a disciple of Christ, and "build and plant" communities of faith.[16]

In Paul Minear's critical study from 1960, *Images of the Church in the New Testament*, he seeks to root our understanding of the nature of the church in scripture by reminding us of the many biblical images for the church.[17] This earlier work on the biblical images for the nature of the church reflects the missionary character of the church at every point. Paul Minear discovers more than eighty metaphors imaging the nature of the church. None of these images suggests that the church has as its goal the creation of vocations and the preservation of social and political order. He wrote this work as a challenge to the ecumenical movement's ecclesiology over fifty years ago, but his insights continue to be valid today. This book was offered to the Faith and Order of the World Council of Churches as a challenge to their effort to address the nature of unity of the church.[18] His work argues that there are four main images of the

---

15. Skreslet, *Picturing Christian Witness*, 15ff.

16. Ibid, 37ff.

17. *The Third World Conference on Faith and Order Council*, 15–16. At this seminal event the most basic of ecumenical and conciliar principles was articulated: Christian Churches should "act together in all matters except those in which deep differences of conviction compel them to act separately." This is known as the Lund Principle. The conference was motivated by a deep concern for the way to measure Christian unity and the call to discipleship.

18. Paul Minear, a biblical scholar teaching at Yale Divinity School, was imbued with the ecumenical spirit of the times. He was a member of the Commission on Faith and Order, a founding member of The North American Academy of Ecumenists, begun as the Association of Professors Teaching in Ecumenics, and was associated with the *Journal of Ecumenical Studies*.

church: the New Creation, the fellowship of faith, the body of Christ, and the people of God.

Once the use of the neologism "contextual theology" came into play, Paul Minear made his own proposal for doing theology within a faithful Christian community. In 1976 he wrote an essay entitled "Theology—Vocation or Profession," a compact and concrete contribution to understanding the means for doing theology among all the churches of the globe as this task has been impacted by modernity. Biblical images of the nature of the church and of vocations within Christian life are key resources for a deeper approach to Christian reflection, surpassing the more abstract theologies of Christendom. He argues that a good theologian permits their "perspectives of thought and action to be controlled by the revelation of God's ultimate judgment and mercy . . . he can develop a 'situational theology' more akin to 1 Peter than to that of his secular colleagues." The theologian is enabled to "orient his vocation around the mission of the church until he recognizes that one hope which is anchored in the work of the Triune God. At all these points the New Testament would contribute to his ability to be a Christian theologian, and to give a faithful accounting of the one hope that inheres in our vocation" to do theology.[19]

Paul Minear's point was that the real nature of the theological vocation is disguised when theology is understood as a profession within an institutional structure like the academy. Theologians, in order to recover their vocation, need to do theology in contact with the realities experienced by the church today, where the means for contact are brought into confrontation with these realities through the power of biblical insight. Reflection on past experience and the doctrinal traditions they established forces theological reflection into habitual and inherited patterns of thinking, which could distort the pastoral and prophetic vocation of the theologian as Christ's faithful disciple.

Around the same time and in a similar vein other theologians chimed in with their own proposals. For example, Gustaf Aulen, Professor at Lund and one of the leaders of the Faith and Order Conference of the

---

19. Paul Minear, "Ecumenical Theology," 15. The reference to 1 Peter is to the study of 1 Peter initiated by the Faith and Order Commission in 1971. This essay was originally a lecture given at Bossey Ecumenical Institute in 1973. The purpose of the studies proposed by the Faith and Order Commission was to create a forum for dialogue concerning the hope of the Christian faith, as it was understood from the differing perspectives of Christians from member churches around the world.

Swedish Lutheran tradition, focused on the metaphors of the church as a body, a plant, and a building, in developing his ecclesiology. Biblical metaphors, stories, and wisdom, Paul Minear and Gustaf Aulen argued, provide us helps for a theological understanding of the nature of the church that call for contextualization. That the Bible is replete with images reflects its canonical nature as an authority for Christian belief and practices—as the measure for authentic living and believing.

Debate on this issue was vitalized by a discussion concerning the form of Christian unity at the Conference of Lund. At that time, the ecumenical movement focused on the one image of Christ. The notion was that the church is built upon the fullness of Christ in history, that is, the meaning of Christ in history. In 1952 the Conference of Lund proposed that the basis of the church be understood as the event of Christ. Christ is the church's center and reality. At the heart of this proposal is the belief in the fullness of the church as seen in Jesus Christ.[20] The focus had shifted from ecclesiology to Christology, distancing theological reflection from the struggles and realities of people. It was believed that common ground had to be found that could lead to ecumenical agreement. The belief in the centrality of the atonement, a foundational doctrine for traditional Christendom and its ecclesial practices, prejudiced the discussion so that the older paradigm of Christology and the work of Christ as atonement, flattened the domain of Christian reflection to the traditional loci of the orthodox European churches. Yet some, such as Paul Minear, sensed that common ground was not enough to ensure a future for ecumenical vision. Common process would be needed that retrieved the importance of context, the vitality of the traditioning process and the cultural power of experience.[21] This process would be enriched by contextual methods, necessary for the integrity of Christian theology.

20. See Jürgen Moltmann's critique of this trend in his book, *Trinity and the Kingdom*. In this book he describes the church as the community of freedom. His social doctrine of the Trinity provides the framework for his argument.

21. This topic has been further developing by Dale Irvin in his *Christian Histories, Christian Traditioning*, 4, 43–44, and 51. Dale Irvin's interesting book attempts to "work from the perspective of contextual theology," so that he can uncover what it means to "contextualize tradition." In so doing he has provided valuable help for those who would encourage the use of contextual methods in promoting healthy traditioning processes. His definition of the use of contextual methods in theology is succinct. He writes, "To contextualize is to argue for boundaries, limitations, and the particular. It is to seek after the localized form, or the particular incarnation in which and through which the enduring truth of life might flow," ibid., 4.

The majority voice of the Conference of Lund argued that the Christ event contains all that we need to know about the nature of the church and its mission in the world. The basis of the argument is that all churches, no matter what model they follow, confess that Jesus Christ is Lord. Ecclesiology dissolves into Christology. In proclaiming that Jesus is the Christ, the church declares that it follows Jesus Christ and becomes embodied in him. Disciples of Christ no longer ask what is true and right, but look to Christ for the answers to these questions. The church is a corporate body in the Spirit of Christ. It is dependent upon its head (Christ, its only true Shepherd) for its direction. The church is not an autonomous institution, but a theonomous community of the faithful. As its members embody Christ in their lives and their life together it moves forward as the living witness to Christ.

The argument is sound, but weak. Adductive reasoning allows us to bring into question the flatness of this position and to imagine a bigger picture that draws people into the narrative of the gospel so their lives are directly involved.[22] This is certainly one image from the New Testament of the church. Yet, it is not helpful to conflate all potential understandings of the nature of the church in relation to Christ's embodiment in the world. Scripture did not. The richness of the biblical story offers images waiting to come alive in the church. This reality has implications for the concrete life of church. From its beginning contextual theology has decried the poverty of the approach that locates theological solutions as answers to particular intellectual problems. By including contextual methods it opens all formative elements for belief and practice, that is all images and doctrines and their language of faith, to the possibility of integrating faith within the lives of local congregations and faith communities.

To see the promise of this approach, let us look at some of these images detected as central by Paul Minear in his study. The image of

---

22. Abduction, according to C. S. Peirce, is reasoning that infers answers to philosophical and scientific problems based not primarily on induction (observation) or deduction (a priori principles), but upon the natural capacity of the human mind to imagine theories of reality based upon the limits and possibilities of appropriate hypotheses. According to C. S. Peirce such reasoning is the best way to explain intellectual skill and pragmatic problem solving, that is, the ability to make sense of this world. Similarly Thomas Kuhn and Imre Lakatós have shown the shallowness of trying to make sense of the world based on foundationalist logic—that is of arguments based upon induction and deduction. Foundationalist logic is not enough.

the vine, he states, is one of the most important images in the New Testament. In this image Christ is the source of the life and existence of the church. Here its creation, existence, and reality depend upon him for it is Christ who sustains the faithful. Another image is that of the church as a building or temple. Here the church is not built with hands but with faith. In brief, the Christian life is impossible without the church. Another image comes from the prophetic tradition; it is the image of the church as the cornerstone. Accordingly, the only way that God can be known is within the building. This image gave form to the doctrine that there is no salvation outside of the church. This doctrinal tradition is ancient, being espoused by theologians from Cyprian to John Calvin, being generally advocated by every ecclesial tradition from the earliest days of Christianity until today, throughout the world. Here the one who has God as father has the church as mother.[23] This tradition gives rise to another; that the mission of the church is to proclaim the lordship of Christ over heaven and earth. Here the lord is the Messiah and our age is messianic. The church accordingly awaits with an active expectation the coming of the Lord, who will come again and bring down the curtain of creation. Use of this image affirms the eschatological framework of history and of the church in the context of the kingdom. It strengthens the conviction that those who believe in Jesus are saved and will have eternal life.[24] How we interpret this traditional doctrine says a great deal about our understanding of the true church.

As Paul Minear, in his book on the *Images of the Church in the New Testament*, uncovers images of the church in the New Testament, we can see how they engage us as Christians.[25] They become mediators of Christian wisdom. Imagery is not determinative of doctrine, but it does connect us, through the experience of the church in a particular context and point to the history of the faithful. Having found the faithful, we can take our place among them by being good Christians in our place and time. Images are ways that the church has expressed its identity. They are revelatory for the community of the faithful that believes that their story and God's story are inseparable.

---

23. Braaten, *Mother Church*. This is a contemporary attempt to revive this understanding for the Lutheran tradition.

24. John 14:1ff.

25. Minear, *Images of the Church*, 28–65, 250–67. Minear's discussion of the use of metaphors in the play of culture is relevant and valuable.

In addressing a similar issue, Gerhard Sauter in his essay, "How Can Theology Derive from Experience," in the book *Doing Theology Today*, says, "We must learn in our theology to work at the 'middle distances' instead of settling for nothing less than theological notions" that are too abstract and encompassing. "We can no longer choose for our discussions and theological study programs which sound correct and impressive only because they are in fact meaningless. We must learn to spell out in detail the great words of faith—freedom, hope, love; . . . we must take the risk of expressing them in the form of limited concrete examples and of using these to test together how much creative power they possess, in order, after a while, to begin our questioning afresh." This is the path that can be followed when we allow biblical wisdom to shape our responses and practices, so that we can be connected to the story of faith. Using biblical images of the church can help us construct helpful ecclesiologies. They make good theology possible.

The weakness of contemporary theology among Western churches is connected with its lack of spiritual experience and with its engagement with values and stances of restricted validity and significance for the people of faith. Biblical wisdom is ignored, while battles over issues that are not raised by members of the church rage in theological schools and offices of ecclesial practice. The connection to the limited world of our reality must be constantly revised and preserved. The work of the theologian takes place as the theologian helps the faith community to weave together their ideas and perspectives, empowered by biblical wisdom, so that they become meaningful and coherent for the local church. Theology participates in the small steps we take as we try to figure out how to respond faithfully as Christians, where and when were are.[26] The use of contextual methods can help to make this possible.

IS THERE A FUTURE FOR THEOLOGY AMONG THE "ESTABLISHED" CHURCHES?

Analogous to the weakness of Western theology is the weakness of the church. For many in the West the church is analogous to a domestic—an institution that serves us. Today it has found a niche in the social fabric where it is caught in the weave, unable to have a healthy identity. Secularism realized due to modern disenchantment of our world has

---

26. Sauter, "How Can Theology Derive from Experience?" 81f.

made it possible to create powerful economic markets, while stripping our world of spiritual significance.[27] Weak theology has been complicit in this process. During the era of Christendom, the church became an institution without a mission. Today that vision is close to fulfillment. The denomination has reserved for itself the task of self-preservation. It is often an institution for itself. Yet, a church without mission has lost its apostolic covenant. We are called and sent for mission among all, not for self-service.

In 1976 W. A. Visser't Hooft recognized the danger we were facing. In his article, "Evangelism in the Neo-Pagan Situation," he recognized this problem as a threat to the future of the church.[28] If the church imagines that all that is Western is Christian, it will tolerate the pagan worldview without critique. Pagans are not just modern Christians; they are proposing religious beliefs that render Christian belief powerless. Nietzsche was not just a disgruntled Christian; he was a pagan. In our current situation we are ripe for re-evangelization. We need to be prepared for "doing mission" at home. We need to be prepared to authentically proclaim the gospel anew everywhere.

Lesslie Newbigin made this hope his late career.[29] After he returned from India where he had been a missionary for decades, he discovered a West desperately in need of the gospel. As noted earlier, the missionary movement, which had accompanied colonialism, had brought the world the gospel; but it had been understood as an expansion of Western culture. Its success, however, perpetuated and shared the influence of the Enlightenment.[30] Those who heard the gospel from nineteenth century missionaries often could not distinguish the uniqueness of the gospel from a belief in the superiority of Western technology, economics, and philosophy. A conviction, that was little short of manifest destiny, wedded mission and colonial ideology. The belief in the Promised Land was often confused with the West as the home of abundant life. Arrogance and sacrifice commingled in a drive to convert and modernize. The deprived peoples of the world were to be provided with progressive religion and Western culture, progress, and technology. The principle became embedded in our imaginations that we were transforming people through

27. Taylor, *A Secular Age*, 513ff.

28. Visser 't Hooft, "Evangelism in the Neo-Pagan Situation," 83.

29. Newbigin, *Foolishness to the Greeks*; Hunsberger, *Bearing the Witness of the Spirit*.

30. Bosch, *Transforming Mission*.

modern medicine, agriculture, education, and religion. This principle remains alive today as a powerful cliché.

In spite of the approach, the modern mission movement was remarkably successful. Yet, the ecclesiology of Western churches was not missional. The church was no longer a missionary church. It was not a response to the love and empowerment of a missionary God. The God of the Christian scriptures and of the early church is a God who was reclaiming the whole of creation—embracing it that it may come under divine rule. Yet, to its eventual loss, the doctrinal traditions of the church lacked references to the eschatological reality of the church's very existence. They lacked references to missional purpose. The existence of the church was not linked to the coming of God's kingdom. The church became a church for itself and not others. This was the point of Dietrich Bonhoeffer's famous declaration that the church must become a church for others if it is to recover its integrity in a secular world.[31] The confessional statements of both the Protestant and Roman Catholic churches were weak and incomplete. They fostered inward ecclesiocentric identities, which naturally forged boundaries and antagonistic belief structures.

Vatican II helped by repositioning ecclesiology as essentially missionary and mission as essentially ecclesial. Today the development of contextual methods in theology and the ecclesiological work initiated by the ecumenical movement and the Roman Catholic Church is rooting the self-understanding of the church in biblical and early church soil.[32] Mission and theology are rightly understood as intertwined. There are no mission fields, because the globe is the place where mission takes place. There was never a biblical basis for the idea. Western developments of political and religious ideology spawned the concept, not biblical wisdom. The gospel is the heart of the Christian life wherever it is lived, and it can live everywhere.

---

31. Dietrich Bonhoeffer made this point in his ethics and ecclesiology. Bonhoeffer discusses the integrity of the church in terms of costly grace in *Discipleship*, 43–56, see esp. p. 53. Costly grace "forgives sins and liberates the sinner." Grace frees us for Christian community. Cf. Bonhoeffer, *Widerstand und Ergebung* (usually translated as *Letters and Papers from Prison*). This point about grace has become an axiom of contemporary missionary theology.

32. Cf. Newbigin, "What is 'a Local Church Truly United?'" 114ff. A helpful summary of the nature of witnessing unity is contained in Newbigin, *Gathered for Life*.

Authentic mission, if it is to be ecclesial, must take into consideration the context of the living church. This implies a role for contextual methods that was not understood in the era of Christendom. We have inherited a great deal from Christendom models of the church that we need to overcome. For North Americans, especially, this will be difficult. The place for authentic contextualization has been filled by remote, individualistic, and manipulative evangelism. North Americans, and with them Christians around the world who have modeled this approach to evangelism, have a long and culturally embedded history with tent and TV evangelism. The populist approach barely touches the cultural and social lives of the people it hopes to convert. It remains superficial. The dominance of populist evangelists is contrasted with the powerlessness of the evangelistic efforts made by local churches. This vacuum is being filled by the rise in interest in mission by local churches, especially among the young. Yet his vacuum has left a terrible legacy.

Another problem arising from the dominance of Christendom models of the church is the critical enervation of Western theology. Due to the power of the traditions of Western political philosophy, so deeply rooted in the religious traditions of the West, Christianity accommodated modernity without learning from it. It succumbed to its failings for it lacked the courage of its convictions about eschatology and divine purpose. How likely is it that we will see the same thing happen with the pitfalls of post-modern approaches to reality? In both cases, of modernity and post-modernity, the very character of commitment to the truth is different. The mission of the church is to share the truth of the gospel. This cannot be mitigated by modern or post-modern concerns about meta-narratives or misuse of language.[33] If foundationalism and referentialism no longer are helpful, that does not put an end to Christian conviction. Christian theology's starting point is the God of Jesus Christ.

---

33. Rorty, *Philosophy and Social Hope*, 148ff. Rorty shares logical positivism's distrust of religious metaphysics. Yet he believes that such distrust goes too far in delegitimizing all wisdom except scientific wisdom. For Rorty cultural traditions have value in that they can mediate between objective science and historically embedded wisdom articulated in narratives and social norms. Yet, talk of ultimate reality, he argues, is in itself misleading. Our language does not correspond to any version of ultimate reality, let alone that of a transcendent divine reality. Paul Ricoeur's book *Hermeneutics and the Human Sciences* offers a more balanced approach that recognizes the rich value of traditions in settling any moral, political, social, or religious problem.

This is not just our opinion; it is the truth. It claims us and all others at all times and places.

Post-modern epistemological relativism, pragmatism, and political theory alter the territory, but they do not infringe on the truth. Even if language is not referential and cannot be shown to aid in objective talk of reality, Christians cannot and will not give up their belief that their talk of God is rational. Religious language is not just about power relations or sublimation; it is about something that is real. Christian talk is truthful, helpful, and, yes, rational.

Christian theology aids the Christian community by providing means to assess and propose meaningful practices and profound beliefs about God. It affirms the conviction that there are reasons to believe and that some religious and anti- or non- religious beliefs are harmful and unfaithful to reality. The failings of Christendom models have left Christian theology vulnerable to the cultural thrust of pagan philosophical and political thought. A healthy understanding to the relation of the Christian faith to culture and society can provide the immunity the church needs to live out its mission in any context. Christianity always transforms culture as well and finds a home in any culture. We must not allow ourselves to become bogged down by the reality of religious pluralism. The resources of culture alone can never justify Christian beliefs and practices, whether it is according to the demands of Western rationalism and science or non-Western spirituality. In this Karl Barth was correct: no culture, philosophy, or religious tradition can function as the source for the life of the church. Their human spirit cannot become confused with the work of the Holy Spirit.

David Hume, Friedrich Nietzsche, Karl Marx, and Michel Foucault are pagans of Western culture, who continue to lure intellectuals from around the world. Their stances cannot be accommodated, exactly because of the nature of a healthy relationship with culture. We can and should learn from them, but not adopt their convictions concerning the nature of reality. The spiritual genealogy of neo-paganism is old and distinguished, taking us back to Greece, Egypt, and Persia. Every culture harbors forms of belief that cannot and ought not to be accommodated to Christian living—Western, Eastern, Northern, or Southern. The encounter of Christian mission has faced many challenges. No culture can be identified with Christian culture. The transformation that is taking place in the world that is the *missio Dei* is a work in progress.

Post-modern thinking has done little to unravel the identification of Christianity with Western and in many contexts American culture. Both liberals and conservatives around the world continue to act and think according to the social imaginary that blends Christianity with social, political, and scientific progress. In the wonderful cultural diversity of the world, one would imagine that this blend would have come unraveled so that it could not be operative. No matter. God offers the place where you are and all the places in the world as centers for mission. We are to pursue the task to evangelize the world without delay, in spite of the imperfect fit that exists between the reality of God and the world.

It is because of this that contextual methods are vital. If the church is to recover its proper form and identity it must become missional; and to do this it will need to become masterful in its appreciation of cultural diversity and contextual possibility. At the same time we will need to recognize the wisdom embedded in Christian traditions that can make transparent the divine truths of our world and existence. Experience and tradition can enable those addressed by God to respond responsibly to their and our world in ways that are meaningful, truthful and enriching. Receiving and experiencing wisdom, we experience transcendence, which leads not to flight from the world but a return to it and its reality. As we turn now to the impact of contextual methods upon the theology of the new Christianity, we will see this process forging bonds of Christian community across time and space, opening us to the experience of the divine whereby our peace and identity are assured.

2

Contextual Methods within the Theological Processes of Christian Churches

THE REALITY OF A NEW CHRISTIANITY CALLS FOR CONTEXTUALIZATION

MISSIOLOGISTS, SUCH AS LAMIN Sanneh and Andrew Walls, have made it clear that the migratory nature of Christianity is evident today in a dramatic way. We are facing a new Christianity centered geographically, socially, culturally, economically, and politically in environments unfamiliar to the West, such that our theological work is called upon to think creatively in terms of the ideas and cultural life, the beliefs and practices of the churches of the new center.[1] The reality of a new Christianity in the offing is the stimulus for a commitment to an ecumenical and ecclesial theology and praxis of mission. It is the epicenter for new changes in thinking and theological praxis.[2] Our situation calls for a renewed and principled motivation to re-vision the church in biblical, contextual, and missional terms. When mission and ecumenism are conceived in answer to the challenges of our day, the weak ecclesiology and its denominationalism, worn thin by ineffective efforts to secure survival in a dramatically changing situation, will no longer hold sway.

Both the established churches and the evangelical and charismatic churches are changing their understanding of the nature of the church and its mission through spiritual discernment. It is the encounter with

1. Cf. Walls, *The Cross-Cultural Process in Christian History*; Walls, *The Missionary Movement in Christian History*; Sanneh, *Disciples of All Nations*; Sanneh, *Whose Religion is Christianity?*

2. The epicenter's migration has stirred considerable interest. Examples include Jenkins, *The New Faces of Christianity*; Jenkins, *The Next Christendom*; and Noll, *The New Shape of World Christianity*.

the global South and the challenge of secularism that have led to new and deeper awareness of the work of Christian communities. The churches, whether they are accepting of liberation theologies or not, are speaking of fighting for justice and against poverty and oppression. The voices of Christians in the global South are making the difference, as well as a new attitude and motivation to listen on the part of the churches of the West.

Secularism, embedded deeply in the cultures and societies of the West, has taken on different character in less economically developed countries. The weakness of a public sphere and the failure to create healthy market systems have combined with corruption to form governments throughout the Third World that do not serve people. While in the West where the public sphere is strong, people assume that the government will listen to them. In the global South where the public sphere is weak or almost non-existent, there is little pressure for government to listen to their people.[3] The pressure to Westernize seems to leave people no alternative but to take on Western approaches to economic and social life.[4] The transition to nationhood, which was so alluring just a few decades to ago, seems filled with crisis and suffering. The secularization that has resulted has led to corruption and disorder, as well as to more transparent politics and developing markets, especially those aligned with globalization. Yet it has not marginalized religion, as it has in the so-called First World. Just the opposite has taken place.

The rise of secularism in the Third World has given form to public spaces that are permeable. The social institutions and imagination that structure political and social life have not removed religion, as they have in the West. Speaking of Western modernity, Charles Taylor says, it "is secular, not in the frequent, rather loose sense of the word, where it designates the absence of religion, but rather in the fact that religion

3. Taylor, *Modern Social Imaginaries*, 185ff.; Taylor, *A Secular Age*, 185–96; Habermas, *The Structural Transformation of the Public Sphere*.

4. Cf. Berger, "Four Faces of Global Culture," and Berger, "The Cultural Dynamics of Globalization." This has been intensified as globalization has developed bringing the world economy into our homes. One impact of globalization, argues Michel Foucault, and John and Jean Comaroff, appears to be that we are becoming entrepreneurs of ourselves. Cf. Foucault, *Naissance de la biopolitique* and John and Jean Comaroff, *Ethnicity, Inc.*, 51. This is particularly evident in the Third World, where poverty and struggles over ethnic identity have led to dramatic instances of the blending of the biological, the political, and the cultural. The prominence of ethnic conflict is only one element of this development.

occupies a different place, compatible with the sense that all social action takes place in profane time."[5] Although there is pressure to make this shift, social action among most Third World peoples does not take place in profane time. The context of life engagements and responsibilities is different and must be understood as such. The strategy for configuring our theological responsibility well needs to include contextual methods from the beginning. The theological process must make sense within the context of people's lives. In order to discern what is involved in acting and thinking responsibly, we have to include in our theological process methods that will connect Christian wisdom to the struggles of particular people living in specific places, faced with challenges that are theirs.

Globally evangelistic responsibility includes social responsibility. If we focus simply on "spiritual" issues, such as conversion and church growth, we fail to listen to the gospel. Jesus expects us to be disciples, not promoters of an institution. While the goal of sharing the gospel should never be abandoned, a new awareness of the call of faith is bringing about a new commitment to a Christianity embedded in culture and the lives of people. To call people to faith is to call people to follow Christ as members of a community with struggles and unique spiritual and political needs. In the West modernity has forged a domain of political life that assumes a secular displacement of religion, while in the "new Christianity" this is often not the case. To advocate a theological process that ignores this reality is to produce unhealthy churches.

The theological reflection, among communities not culturally embedded in a Western modernity, has led to new decisions concerning the praxis and practices of the church. A broad consensus is developing among Christians from the "new Christianity" that mission cannot be defined in either purely horizontal or vertical terms. A convergence is taking place aligning the faith and belief of Christians from the global South with their beliefs and experiences. The heart of this transformation is a new appreciation of the power of the biblical story.

In the chapter, "Power in the Book," of his book, *The New Faces of Christianity*, Philip Jenkins discusses perspectives of the global South on the authority of the Bible in the life of their churches. He lists new factors that support religious commitment reliant upon the inspiration of sacred texts. I will not repeat his argument here, due to its length. Its points, however, should not be missed. It is important for our argu-

---

5. Taylor, *Modern Social Imaginaries*, 194.

ment, because it supports the claim of many observers of Christianity today that the "new Christianity" interprets the Bible differently from the established and evangelical churches of the West.[6] This movement did not coincide with the advent of Christianity within their nations, but rather in the 1960s. The coincidence was the end of colonial control and the rise of national struggles in the global South. During this decade the first steps reflecting an awareness of the importance of context were also taken.

Jenkins writes, "The Bible did not occupy anything like its central role in the belief or worship of the vast majority of Christians until the second half of the twentieth century. Only in the 1960s did Bible reading acquire its exalted status . . ."[7] The legacy of the theologies of missionaries may have something to do with this, but it is cannot be identified with it. Many "founding" missionaries were conservative, but their approaches to Christian scripture are very different from those found in the communities of the "new Christianity." The factor that acted to catalyze the shift can best be understood in terms of contextuality or contextual reality.

The distinctions that Western theologians found necessary and helpful because they lived in cultures and societies structured by modernity are not found helpful or interesting among non-Western peoples. Context is not just relevant for scholarship; it changes the face of the church. It is the catalyst for conceiving evangelism, social action and mission in partnership.

Roman Catholicism has also renewed its understanding of mission in awareness of the transformations afoot. A renewed authoritative Roman Catholic theology of mission was advanced in *Ad Gentes* or "The Decree on the Missionary Activity of the Church." The affirmation confirmed a biblical understanding of the human condition that emphasized the *missio Dei*. This understanding re-stated for the "new Christianity" the conviction that the gospel, that is the conviction that God acted uniquely in Jesus Christ for the salvation of the world, is the only motive for mission. Mission and evangelism converge in a theology that acknowledges that Christian mission must be conducted as a response to the *missio Dei*. The mission of the church is to participate in what God is doing in the world. This can take the form of church

6. Jenkins, *The New Faces of Christianity*, 18ff.

7. Ibid., 18–19.

planting or of the struggle for justice; but it cannot take place without the church.

Later, John Paul II's papal encyclical, *Ut Unum Sint*, voiced the conviction of Protestants, Evangelicals and Roman Catholics around the world, who believe that mission and evangelism must proceed on an ecumenical basis. Mission can no longer be allied with a particular culture and a particular confessional stance. To do so is to preserve a flawed theology of mission that ignores the cultural and social context of the people with whom we seek to share the gospel. The work of the church is to enable belief in the love and grace of God, so that the world may believe and experience God's love. The work of God to reconcile the world is the will of God and the basis for Christian evangelism. Our divisions and cultural arrogance "thwart the proclamation of the gospel of salvation in the cross of Jesus . . ."[8]

Theological pluralism, which is popular among Western intellectuals, has not been comfortable with this development, although efforts to integrate their convictions have been taken.[9] It is yet to be seen as to whether an ecumenical missiology can accommodate theological

---

8. John Paul II, *Ut Unum Sint*, 2.

9. Some representatives to the Second World Missionary Conference held in Jerusalem in 1928 proposed a revisionist theological pluralism that argued that it was no longer reasonable to believe in the uniqueness of Christ over against the revelatory character of other religions. The exclusivism of faith in Christ was to be abandoned as well as the need to evangelize. An enlightened synthesis based upon a progressive and global philosophy of religion should be adopted. The modern church should abjure any efforts to convert and put its efforts into the new international social order of justice and modern progress, advocated by the Social Gospel. Dietrich Bonhoeffer's essay on this subject was his response to this development: Bonhoeffer, "Memorandum: The Social Gospel," 236ff. Cf. Visser 't Hooft, *The Background of the Social Gospel in America*. Both Bonhoeffer and Visser 't Hooft fault the theology of the Social Gospel for its weak Christology and its shallow understanding of social justice that lacks an eschatological and biblical framework. Lamin Sanneh argues in his recent book, *Disciples of All Nations*, that the policy of the World Council of Churches never rejected revisionist pluralism. This stance continued to be evident at the Conference of the World's Student Christian Confederation at Strasbourg in 1960 (ibid., 272ff.). Nonetheless, the WCC did not lose interest in mission and evangelism, quite the contrary; as is evidenced in its advocacy of contextual methods in theology, and its effort to retrieve the meaning of the doctrine of the Trinity for the contemporary and global church. Lamin Sanneh is not alone in recognizing the debilitating effects of theological pluralism upon the ecumenical movement. Cf. Wainwright, "The Global Structures of Ecumenism," 19. According to Geoffrey Wainwright, the rise of theological pluralist influence among leaders of the World Council of Churches has sidelined their work on mission and evangelism, thus dramatically diminishing their ecumenical voice.

pluralism to the extent that some scholars such as Paul Knitter, John Hick, John Cobb, and Aloysius Pieris insist. Their positions, almost identical with that of such philosophers of modernity as Gottfried Lessing, Gottfried Leibniz, and Ernest Troeltsch, are aligned with the modern Western secular imagination. Why would commitment to a neutralized religiosity engender common mission among churches? Local churches are unrelenting in their commitment to the revelation in Christ in its entirety. Faith in Christ matters in the Third World, even if it does not matter among in the meetings rooms of the American Academy of Religion and the libraries of modern liberal scholarship. Ecumenism, evangelism, and contextual theology carry the burden together that is borne at the rise of the new Christianity.

The ecumenical movement and the development of a healthy contextual theology will shape the future of theology by reviving the biblical images and perspectives that have found their place among the theologies of peoples from different traditions and places on this planet. The result will be richer and more authentic Christian theologies that will prepare the way for the future and guide Christian communities along the difficult path that lies ahead. Ecumenism and contextual theology can help to restore the integrity of Christian practice and enable theology to help local churches instead of burdening them with theologies that "thwart the proclamation of the gospel."

The "new Christianity" is being constructed at the border where the Bible meets the world.[10] There we find scripture and tradition formative of a new and deeper understanding of mission and evangelism. We also discover the church recovering the relationship between worship and community. The light of the gospel shines through the liturgy and practice of faithful communities as they are empowered to become witnessing communities. Their witness enables them to be fed by the feast of reconciliation. The Holy Spirit rekindles passion for evangelism; while theology guides the community bringing the fullness of Christian traditions and biblical reality into play. Even the finest scholarship is unable to convert our enfeebled church members into missionaries of reconciliation and peace. Theology when it rises from ecumenical vision and draws upon contextual reality can do what it is supposed to do.

---

10. Jenkins, *The New Faces of Christianity*, 42ff.

WHY USE CONTEXTUAL METHODS
IN DOING THEOLOGY?

The claim of this book is that contextual theology makes it possible for theology to do what it is supposed to do. Let us now turn to this proposal. In advocating the use of contextual methods, I am advocating something specific about the theological process in church life. To make my point we need to examine the basics of theological work.

What is theology supposed to do and how can contextual theology help? The classical definition of theology is that Christian theology is the critical work of believers as their faith seeks understanding of God. Anselm of Canterbury and Karl Barth summarized this as *faith seeking understanding*. Christian theology first appeared in the context of the Roman Empire, where it sought to respond to the needs of Christian communities in the turbulent atmosphere of Hellenistic and Roman societies. As a consequence, theologians, even today, tend to identify Christian theology with the earliest controversies and their results and interpretations, and not with the struggle of local congregations as they face the challenge of being Christians in the world. Yet, it was this struggle that marked the earliest debates themselves. Historical distance has led to abstraction.[11]

Another traditional argument defines theology as the effort of the church to meet the needs of the faithful to live consistently with the gospel. Theology was tasked with problem-solving the intellectual puzzles of the intellectual critics of Christian faith. To do this it needed to assume the methods of its critics in order to persuade them of the truth. The content of our faith that was deemed relevant was the content that mattered to the culture of Rome and later Europe—its rulers, the kings, and the popes.

The need to be careful about belief and practice has led theologians throughout the history of Christianity to examine the content of faith, its affirmations and professions, in the context within which it is lived. Its witness has been, from the beginning, local and rooted in social mores and culture.[12]

---

11. Sanneh, *Translating the Message*, 56–81, esp. 65–76. Christianity grew quickly along the ground, that is in a context, which opened up for it within Greek and Roman cultures.

12. Bevans, "A Local Theology in a World Church," 86.

Contextualization has been part of the history of faith communities and yet has not always been part of the *methodology* of theological thought. For the most part, cultural patterns have been assumed in the process of making the gospel understandable. The tools to investigate properly for the purposes of theology have been absent. It is possible to observe contextualization throughout Christian history, but the turn to contextual *methods* is new. We are newly attuned to the need for contextual methods, because the global reality of Christianity's reach is now compelling us to study and discern more fully an authentic process by which knowledge of God can be communicated. The social reality of peoples around the world is being transformed in dramatic ways. Globalization, for example, is impacting communities everywhere, establishing new relationships and economic pressures initiating a tectonic shift in daily life. Today communities throughout the world are impacted by a variety of cultural and economic realities that are extending flows of power and knowledge. New challenges ensue. Because less than authentic processes have been used in the past, such as coercion and economic incentives, the integrity of the faith has been tarnished and the quality of the Christian life corrupted. Contextual methods are proposed in order to overcome the impact of disingenuous processes.

With this hope in mind, faith communities are doing contextualizing theology humbly. Christian theology uses contextual methods once the theologian discerns what can be known about God and then communicates this knowledge to a particular community. The two steps are integrated, because the meaning of the first step can only be discerned as a truth having ultimate value for a person and a believing community in a particular time and place. The second step is the fulfillment of the first, for it enacts the intent of the first step, which is to believe and practice belief in God. Contextual methods must be applied here to use language that can bear meaning in a particular context. In the process of communicating the message, knowledge of context is vital. Good theology happens, I argue, when the theological process embeds the gospel message in the cultural memory of a particular community. This is the means by which biblical wisdom can be a resource for the beliefs and practices of Christian communities and believers. Historical, cultural and social realities need to be seen as essential elements of the events that create and transform the identity and experiences of people. Therefore, we should construct interpretations of cultural life that help us to do theology responsibly.

To accomplish this some theologians have abstracted the process of communicating the gospel from the theological process and defined mission in terms of this process. According to this argument, Christian theology is simply the exercise of defining what needs to be communicated, the *regula fidei*; and mission is the mediation or communication of the content of Christian belief. Yet is contextual theology simply a method of explanation? However much contextual theology involves translation, it is not only a method for communicating the gospel. One does not just find the correct translation and publicize it, as Eugene Nida suggests.[13] This would equate mission and communication. Christians, in this model, are like relay stations. They receive and transmit the gospel. Here cultures are like isolated wholes or systems—a position that contemporary anthropology has abandoned. Here mission is simply the process of translating from one system to another. There is little more to it. The difference between the sender and the receiver is, however, an essential part of the Christian life and the formation of Christian community. To conflate communication and mission is to crush the life out of the theological process. Christian theology is not a one-dimensional form of mediation between individuals. Theology is a process that is only complete within the act of witness and reconciliation with God and neighbor.

Other theologians have argued that contextual theology is a new vision for community life that becomes concrete within the process of history. Here, as Gustavo Gutierrez, J. B. Metz, and Roger Haight have argued, life is the context for Christian commitment, belief, and spirituality. The process of theology is conflated into a response to the experience of love concretized in movements of freedom within history. These experiences open us to the liberation God made possible in Christ. Experience of God illumines human life. The end result of the theological reflection of those advocating this argument is a vision of the Christian life. According to J. B. Metz and other liberation theologians, the reality of modern secularization leaves the church no choice but to conceive mission as political action in the cause of freedom from domination. Because life is violated by human domination, we should participate in political movements that will transform this situation. Otherwise true spirituality is rendered impossible by the political reality of domination. Mission and with it the process of contextualization in

13. Nida, *Message and Mission*; Nida and Reyburn, *Meaning across Cultures*.

theology are elements of responsible action (praxis) for the world in the hope of transformation.[14]

Should contextual theology have the primary goal of developing a spiritual vision of freedom for the community of faith? Certainly living a faithful life guided by the love of God and neighbor issues in a vision that is an alternative to that prior to knowledge of God.[15] Yet the truth about the God who redeems is important. Without faith in God the faith in transformation is shallow in significance. If political action is the goal of theological reflection then there is no role for the church or for evangelism. The church has no mission, because the mission is essentially political. The reason for the failure to develop a theology that is relevant for Christian churches is the improper use of contextual methods. Here the formative conviction is that the contemporary situation is one of political domination. Domination results as new structures are formed due to secularization and globalization. These statements form the core convictions and starting point of their methodical structure. This is a highly abstract generalization that does not begin to struggle with the problems of local communities of faith. Liberation theologians abandon abstract metaphysics only to replace it with abstract political theology. Both are vulnerable to theory damaging revision, as they have been whenever contextual methods have been poorly valued. For example, J. B. Metz's secularization theory has been shown to be disingenuous, for he fuses the secular and sacred so that sacred institutions lose their identity.[16] Theologians who rely upon modern theory are all too often disappointed.

The problem of this approach is that it defines the church in political terms and not in terms of its contextual reality, thus preserving the

---

14. Cf. Rütti, *Zur Theologie der Mission*, 345; Metz, *Theology of the World*. Rütti and Metz reject Vatican II's decree on mission (*Ad Gentes*), because they do not see the goal of mission in ecclesial terms, but in terms of political action. According to them, the experience of forgiveness of sin and the experience of the empowerment of the Holy Spirit do not led to the duty to change the world and are therefore irrelevant to the present situation.

15. Haight, *An Alternative Vision*, 8, 239ff.

16. Cf. Taylor, *Secular Era*, 332–51, 570–74. Charles Taylor rejects the argument that secularization is a recession of religion in the face of science. The argument of Metz proposes that modern science and political theory emerge to liberate us from the tutelage of capitalism and the complicity of ecclesial institutions with oppression. Taylor argues against positions like those of Metz that support a progressive humanism. He believes that the bald contrast of religion and science, secular and sacred, was a chimera.

separation of church and political life. The contextual method they use is insufficient and flawed. They seek to bridge the political and theological by use of a socio-analytic mediation. The error they make is to divide the ecclesial and political in the first place. In the local church, faith is a political and loving engagement for the benefit of others; it is a strike against the sinful forces of this world. The "true church of the poor" is simply the true church, not a branch of a left-wing political organization. A church is not just a community of cheerleaders for justice. Such an understanding of the church does not empower resistance to corrupt capitalism or brutal governments, for example. Contextual theology does not just mediate between the theological and the political, it engenders the political through faith, by countering oppression and rendering the distortion of sinful living powerless. Good theology heals a broken world by countering political distortions of life and forming a way of life arising from faith in Christ. Liberation theologies believed that they could provide the church with a helpful contextual interpretation of the current condition of human living, but they failed to provide a substantive ecclesiology that recognizes the practice of faith as intrinsically political, social, cultural, and economic. Good theology refuses to be just another interest group participating in the public sphere. It is a public in its own right.[17]

Love is not an abstract value that needs to be translated—mediated—into politics. Love is something formed within the quotidian of everyday struggles and challenges, as people try to be Christians where and when they are.[18] Theology is not for the academy; the academy is for the theology that is living in the world. Theology is for the church and the world.

This is why contextual theology is so important at this moment in human history. Contextual methods call us to take seriously the problems that churches are facing in trying to be Christian in a world and time like ours. These problems are no longer simply metaphysical and

17. Milbank, *Theology and Social Theory*, 413. Milbank tries to tempt us with the notion that Augustine argued for a social realm where the "complex and interlocking powers" of church and state intermingle and render a dominant state or a hierarchal and conformist church from colluding with injustice.

18. Augustine of Hippo frequently made the point that the love of the church and the love we have for one another are inseparable. Together they form the root of the unity and mission of the church. This is a point not lost on Lesslie Newbigin and Lukas Vischer. Cf. Vischer, *Intercession*, 57ff.

political; they are religious, spiritual, cultural, economic, social, cosmological, ethical, political, ontological, and environmental. In order to take seriously the respect for human living, the theologian cannot avoid those conditions that matter in making sense of life. Christian faith leads to contextual theology. The process of interpreting the impact on living of those quotidian realities that threaten and engender life entails a full theological engagement with reality and the human condition.

The definition of theology as faith seeking understanding entails the formation of Christian doctrine according to the purposes of God for humanity and the world. Contextualization dusts off old theories for the purpose of retrieving their wisdom for a new community of believers. Therefore, contextualization leads to new theological insights and forms, exactly because it impacts the stories of peoples of faith. Christian theology is not archeology. Uncovering the past is not enough. Theology participates in the new life that comes from knowing God and living according to God's purposes now and for the fulfillment of the future God is preparing for the world. Responsible theology uses contextual methods as the theological process participates in the new life God makes possible. Contextual theology rises in importance when theologians recognize that theology is, by its very nature, done in context. It connects us to the past, the present and the future and reflects upon God's purposes in the context of time. To use theological insights from the past alone is to be unrealistic. It leads to theology that is unhealthy for the church, by perpetuating "hierarchical" church order that colludes with the order of political structures and their dominion.

The world of theological debate reflects the world we live in, connected globally and conflict ridden. Earlier theology did not always face this level of fragmentation, nor did it face a world where the activity of God was so much in question, either due to the skepticism of secularism or in the face of the pain of theodicy. Perspectives on the activity and the inactivity of God shape and deconstruct our understanding of the way that God shapes faithful communities.

THE SUBJECTIVE WITHIN THE THEOLOGICAL PROCESS

The most influential study of contextual theology as applied to mission theory is that of Steven Bevans. He does not focus on the theological process, but rather upon models of contextual theology illustrated by the works of contemporary theologians. Bevans organizes the different approaches to contextualization according to models distinguishable according their approaches to contextuality. His approach assumes that the turn toward contextual theology is a result of the rising awareness of the importance of culturally shaped experience in evangelism and mission.

His book *Models of Contextual Theology* is a text studied around the globe and especially by theological educators working in the Third World. He organizes his material in terms of models for doing theology, using examples from contemporary theology as invitations to do contextual theology. We will not examine all of his models here; although we will take a look at two of his proposals focusing on the contextual methods he sees at play, in order to learn from them and discern the contours of his argument. I will argue that the weakness of the approach is his focus on religious experience. The study of contextual methods is not a buffet, from which you choose the most attractive version according to your experience. Contextual theology is marked by a clear connection to local realities. This is sometimes lost sight of in the process of marking off the characteristics of theologies based upon their efforts to integrate indigenous religious experience in their proposals. Yet, Bevans' work is the most influential to date. It provides helps for mission workers and evangelists as they seek to apply contextual methods to their work. It stimulates discussion about the role of contextual theology in contemporary theology by identifying the marks of contextual methodologies.

Stephen Bevans takes a stand. He believes that theology is subjective before it is objective. Accordingly, theological work is the mission of the church, conducted because religious believers experience God. It is to account for experiences, both past and present, that the church appropriates what it has received and passes it on through witness and profession. The assumption is that the church gains insights from their experience. The simplicity of this approach is both its advantage and its disadvantage. Good theology, he argues, needs to take account of faith experiences of the past and of the present, which he defines as the context.[19] He uses descriptive models to help the practitioner to discern the options open.[20] To narrowly define context in terms of past experience does weaken his theory, for traditional theology was also contextual theology, but it helps to focus on a most relevant topic for mission workers—the present experience of those they seek to serve.

19. Bevans, *Models of Contextual Theology*, 5ff.
20. Ibid., 28ff.

The models, he proposes, differ in their approach according to the four vital concerns common to every contextual theology, but weighted differently according to model. These four concerns are the Kerygma, which he defines as the spirit and message of the gospel, the Christian traditions, the cultures, and the social change within culture or praxis. The articulation of these concerns within the different theologies provides guidelines for distinguishing the different models and evaluating the appropriateness of a theology. In his latest revision, he discerns six models for doing contextual theology, listed here along a spectrum from the least culturally invasive to the doctrinally most specific: the anthropological model, the transcendental model, the praxis model, the synthetic model, the countercultural model, and the translation model. The spectrum runs from those models that are specific about what needs to be added to the cultural life of new believers and what needs to be encouraged within the culture when the gospel is shared. According to Bevans, this spectrum mirrors the basic tension of contextual theology. The tension between the sources for theology rooted in our experience of the present (human experience, culture, social location and change) and in our experience of the past (scripture and tradition).[21] Each model pictures this process differently according to its understanding of how the gospel is shared with integrity. The central problem is the character of the relationship of the gospel and culture—broadly and narrowly conceived. Bevans' proposals, like those of H. R. Niebuhr decades earlier, have shaped the discussion of mission theology in recent years. There are other vital questions at stake as well. These will become clear as we discuss them.

Stephen Bevans' main point about the contribution that contextual theology intends to make is that, in contrast to earlier confessional theologies, contemporary contextual theology takes into account human experience.[22] Traditional theologies, by which he means Roman Catholic doctrinal theologies, sought to develop "a corpus of dogmas that were universally valid no matter what the context." Today, we must not only use the resources of scripture and tradition to construct theology, but also take seriously the context of human experience, and therefore include the contributions and critiques of culture, history, and contempo-

---

21. Bevans, *An Introduction to Theology in Global Perspective*, 171.
22. Bevans, *Models of Contextual Theology*, 1ff.

rary thought, in our theological work.[23] This reveals his orientation as a Roman Catholic scholar who is attempting to struggle with the insights of modern thinking after Vatican II.

Stephen Bevans acknowledges his bias towards contextual theology by affirming that theology is not "only objective but subjective."[24] His position is modernist and humanist. Modernism, on the whole, turns to the human person as the source of reality and the origin of rational knowledge. It is a turn from God being the origin of knowledge and truth to experience being the source of knowledge and truth. Some have called this the turn to human autonomy as the foundation of human rationality. According to Stephen Bevans, the modern turn implies that reality is mediated by cultural meaning. Theology, in that it claims to discern reality, must therefore be concerned with cultural meaning and symbolism, as well as social knowledge and power structures. Because our cultural and historical reality contributes significantly to our construction of reality, our context provides valuable resources for a truthful understanding of God.

By way of contrast, Paul Hiebert, an evangelical scholar, considers contextual methodologies necessary as long as they are aligned with insights of contemporary anthropology.[25] He proposes that it is the worldview that must change in order for the church to be shaped and/or renewed. Consequently, he focuses on personal change made possible through understanding culture. He defines mission and evangelism in subjective categories, focusing on cognitive transformation, affective transformation, and evaluative transformation.[26] Culture is what makes an understanding of reality possible, so that we can experience the world in a meaningful way. It is the Christian faith that provides the coherence we need to make sense of our world. Culture provides the resources to embed in a worldview the truth about God communicable through scripture and tradition. Hiebert's position contrasts with Bevans by isolating the contextual and subjective nature of theological reflection and mission from Christian doctrine, in order to preserve the separation of practice and belief. His goal is the laudable, but limited, goal of overcoming cognitive dissonance so that belief is enabled.

23. Ibid.
24. Ibid.
25. Hiebert, *Gospel in Human Contexts*.
26. Hiebert, *Transforming Worldviews*, 312ff.

Stephen Bevans, on the other hand, believes that contextual theology has a unique contribution as a moment within modern theology. While the call to contextual theology has not led to a new movement, it has been a catalyst for theologies that are as different as the ideologies and cultures of their home of origin.

INCULTURATION, INDIGENIZATION, AND ACCULTURATION

Roman Catholic mission studies have long identified the means of sharing the gospel as the issue to be resolved.[27] The problem identified is inculturation. It is to share the gospel in a form whereby it can be meaningful to those from another culture (or generation). Aylward Shorter, one of the chief exponents of the theology of inculturation, describes it as the culturally compatible sharing of the gospel rendered possible through a mutually enriching encounter between peoples.[28] It is more than acculturation, which denotes the mere interaction between cultures. Acculturation as "the encounter between one culture and another," leads to a cultural learning process, whereby cultures learn from each other.[29] Acculturation is simply encounter; it is not a critical symbiosis that has integrated the experience of Christian revelation within the worldview of another culture. Inculturation, argues Shorter, is mission and/or evangelization, which is identified as a historical process by which Christian beliefs and practices are entered into another cultural worldview and transform that culture. The goal is for beliefs to be held.

The assumption of inculturation is that both the culture and the gospel can co-exist in a mutually enriching way. This is the position of Pope Paul VI in the papal letter called *Evangelii Nuntiandi*. Churches involved in the missionary process of intercultural communication are renewed and enriched. Through intercultural communication, called inculturation, the communion of the church is constituted, uniting the local particular church to the Church Universal.

Is this assumption justified? In so far as culture provides the means for communication, inculturation is vital to any theory of the use of contextual methods and, consequently any theology of mission or evange-

---

27. Cf. Second Vatican Ecumenical Council, *Ad Gentes Divinitus*.

28. Shorter. *Toward a Theology of Inculturation*, 10ff.

29. ibid., 7, 14.

lism. However, the identification of contextualization with inculturation is shortsighted. Culture is one element of context. The context referred to in the proposal for the use of contextual methods is the quotidian and refers therefore to more than culture. This is true for theologies of mission that identify ethnicity and/or religious worldviews as the dominant element of contextual theology.

The process referred to as inculturation is sometimes known as the cultural and historical process by which the gospel becomes expressed in forms proper to a particular culture and thereby promoting processes and events that are faithful both to the particular culture and the gospel. In this process, the communicator seeks to preserve the integrity of the gospel, while the receiver seeks to preserve their identity in the event of listening to the message. This is perceived as a tug-of-war representing the tension between the two cultures. Mission has been reduced to effective interpersonal communication. The appropriateness of the message is evaluated in terms of the local cultural codes. While these codes are important, it is hard to imagine that these codes will not be transformed in some sense during conversion or the renewal of faith.

Inculturation, as well, is sometimes referred to as a variety of indigenous theology. Indigenous theology is theology of a particular people, with geographical, cultural, and social boundaries; it is local in the sense of being identifiable with the theological work, beliefs, and practices of a particular people. Inculturation is reduced, by some, to indigenization where the goal for the receivers of the gospel is to be able to say that the faith that they have received belongs to them. At the end of the process of inculturation the beliefs and practices of Christian conviction have become indigenous.

The theology of mission motivates ecclesiology. If we take contextual theology seriously our ecclesiology is deepened as we rely upon an encompassing understanding of culture. Yet just how encompassing can it be and still reflect reality? Does it denote all that is real for a particular society? Such an understanding is certainly too broad. Culture is the medium for the passing on (sharing) of the gospel from one culture to another, from one generation to another, from one community to another. It does not imply that all that is necessary for a people to grasp the truth is to search the treasures of their culture. Culture is the means for communication not the treasure trove itself. For this reason inculturation is the process whereby the church preserves its reason for being through the sharing of the gospel effectively and appropriately.

Stephen Bevans characterizes the model of inculturation as a form of adaption or translation and calls it the translation model.[30] In this model, mission is imagined to be facilitated through a translation of the gospel message into a new cultural and social reality. The image he uses is that of a kernel and a husk. The gospel is something irreducible that must be translated into the new culture, and the husk is all that is inessential and that ought to be culturally jettisoned in the process. The gospel is something new in every culture and historical human context.[31] Yet it can take root if "translated" and made at home in another culture.

According to Bevans another approach to using contextual methods in theology is the anthropological model. This model follows a humanist tradition. According to this model Christianity is identified with religious and spiritual fulfillment and growth. Human authenticity and spiritualities are at its center. Presupposed is the belief that alone the experience of the ordinary cultural subject is the locus of the manifestation of culture. Each culture instantiates human flourishing or it would not survive; so there is something fundamentally valuable and true in each culture's worldview. Not everyone agrees with this assessment. Spiritual growth and the indigenous sources that make it imminent are but the only distinctive issues at hand. This is myopic.

This model also encourages a process of indigenization, yet it does not seek to introduce something new to the culture, but to develop and enrich the spiritual resources that are *already present*. This model is marked by indigenization characterized by solidarity with the people for their benefit. Such theology is shaped by the culture and the moment in history. It is not contextual theology in the sense advocated with the contextual methods of Paul Lehmann or Shoki Coe. The method here is to promote the spiritual culture of peoples by insuring that there is no intervention from external sources. Theology occurs as mutual encouragement of inviolable religious worldviews. Muriel Montenegro from the Philippines is an example of just such an approach to contextualization.[32]

30. Bevans, *Models*, 37–53.

31. Ibid., 52f.

32. Orevillo-Montenegro, *The Jesus of Asian Women*, 41ff. Her argument sees little value in contextualization. Because religious plurality should be encouraged, she asserts, no attempt to transform religious worldviews or convictions should be made. Inculturation and contextualization should not be attempted, she concludes. Theologians should become advocates of local religious worldviews and ethnic spiritualities.

It is difficult to see why it could be called contextualization, in that there is nothing to contextualize. The religious symbols and practices of the culture are the sole resources for spiritual renewal.

Graced by culture and enriched by faith the theologian using anthropological methods searches what is good and meaningful and uses these to construct a theology for the people. Only those whose worldview is that of the culture at hand can construct such theology. Search out what is good, and address the ethnic problems at hand. Faith is enriched within ones own culture; for it is within ones own culture that God is at work. Promote spirituality that is indigenous.

EATWOT has provided a better approach to this model by terming it an "ethnographic model" and not a model of contextual theology. EAWOT recognizes that it is a method among others, and not the basis for the only approach for all good theology—although there are certainly those who argue that it is. The focus here is on cultural identity and the preservation of this identity as a particular people shapes Christianity.

This trajectory emphasizes a tradition associated with Roman Catholicism and doctrines of creation that emphasize sacramental reality. It focuses the work of theology on the plural religious reality of particular cultures, thus affirming the grandeur of God present in all cultures. Because it is culture that shapes the way faith is articulated, it is culture that determines the content of belief.[33] As Robert McAffee Brown argued in response to the proposal of the 70s to use contextual methods in theology, "context affects content."

The narrowing of this approach tends to encourage theories of reality that are abstract, by making human goodness the prior criterion of theology, and that rely upon universal philosophical presuppositions founded upon theories of human nature and its religious traits. While one may be able to argue that the human being is by nature religious, I do not think it is possible to defend the argument that all religious behavior and belief can be defended according to Christian principle. It also implies that the gospel arises from a concrete situation without intervention from extra-cultural sources. This is something that I do not believe happens. For this reason, this model cannot be seen as a model for theology, but simply an element of good contextual methodology, which without translation is impossible. This method, when practiced alone, focuses exclusively on the present, without recognition of the past.

---

33. Bevans, *Models*, 57–58; Brown, "The Rootedness of All Theology," 170–74.

This is a serious failing, sufficient to be the cause for rejection of any theology that claims to follow the anthropological model in detail.

The narrow focus of this model limits the concern of the theologian to the uniqueness of particular cultures. It is not interested in the interaction between or the insights that may be gleaned from other traditions and cultures, nor does it allow for the possibility that Christian revelation concerning God could be true and helpful to everyone. The basic conviction here is the ultimate value of local religious beliefs and practices.

According to this model, mission results from reflection upon the sacred reality of a particular culture. This reflection is then used as the basis for a theological construction that makes it possible to encourage religious life in a particular society. The missionary is then a midwife within this process. The goal is to assist at the birth of a culturally unique theology. Assumed is the theologically grounded belief that the Word of God has been hidden in the life of a particular culture from the beginning of time. The history of this idea can be found in the early church, when it sought to identify the presence of the divine in the culture of the Roman Empire. At the end of the Roman Empire this was broadened to reinforce the claim of the identification of the presence of the divine within Christendom. Now the view has been broadened to argue that the divine is present in the development of all cultures.

A method that can be used within a contextual theology that seeks to follow this path is meta-linguistic analysis. Meta-linguistic analysis can be used to get at the heart of the sacred reality of a particular culture. This method seeks to locate the spiritual character of a unique cultural reality and promote the incarnation of the Word of God that lies within. Meta-linguistic analysis studies the language used by a people to speak about God's presence. This can be very helpful in attempting to communicate Christian beliefs and practices to people.

This model is particularly valuable for those who believe in the sacramental character of the world. For them revelation is fundamentally a personal encounter with God's love and power in the midst of everyday life. Such theologians believe that scripture and tradition consist in a "history of local theologies," which are not unique amongst other religions.[34] The engagement of communities around the world in globally

---

34. Bevans, *Models*, 59. This critique is joined by Robert Schreiter in his *Constructing Local Theologies*, 14. Cf. Schrieter, *The New Catholicity*.

connected cultural, economic, social, and political processes renders this model naïve. The world has become complex and cannot be conceived according to the heuristic models of modern anthropology, which pictured cultures as hermetic wholes. Acculturation, the fruitful interaction of cultures and religious life, is central to contemporary cultural anthropology. This model uses social science that is no longer accepted by the disciplines that developed them.[35]

BEYOND INCULTURATION: INTERCULTURAL HERMENEUTICS WITHIN THE THEOLOGICAL PROCESS

As noted earlier, contextualization is a recent neologism created in response to the need to encourage the development of ecumenical theological formation. The term arose partly in dissatisfaction with indigenization, adaptation, and accommodation, as used in mission studies at the time, and partly as a response to the lack of theological methodology appropriate to the post-colonial realities of the Third World and the emergence of globalizing secularism.[36] Indigenous methods that promote inculturation and translation methods that promote intercultural communication were studied in order to improve the theology of the ecumenical movement as well as that of the Third World.

Paternalism was viewed as the chief obstacle. Prior to the emergence of contextual methods in theology, translation tended to lack theological theory, and failed to be more than a translation of theology without a clear understanding of the context. Lamin Sanneh's book *Translating the Message* is a catalyst for more effective contextual theology that takes translation to the construction of theology for communities of the new Christianity.[37]

Paul Lehmann noted in his proposal for contextual theology that the use of contextual methods promises to humanize theology. Humanization in this sense refers to the end of theological arrogance, which promotes paternalism in matters of ecclesial and societal authority. Just as theology, that seeks to articulate its practices and beliefs with integrity, must abandon claims to be the queen of the sciences, it

35. Tanner, *Theories of Culture*; and Brown, et al, eds., *Converging on Culture*.

36. Newbigin, *The Gospel*, 42.

37. Sanneh, *Translating the Message*, 192ff. The paternalistic efforts of missionaries were often overturned through vernacular translation.

also must take seriously and humbly its task of service to the church. Christians cannot claim that they do not learn from culture, how to do theology well.[38] In addition contextual methods prevent the church from the "theologization of the human," that is the failing of Christian theologies which do not distinguish God's mission in the world from our very best efforts to transform the world for the better. Contextual theology acknowledges from the beginning that true mission is God's mission and our mission is appropriate only in alignment with what God is doing in the world. In this sense, perhaps Ernest Käseman is correct in pronouncing in response to the demythologization project of Rudolf Bultmann, that the "Apocalyptic was the mother of all Christian theology."[39] The dismissal of the context of the New Testament as irrelevant by modern and existentialist theologians, he argued, was tantamount to dismissing the framework of belief and practice of early Christians. When we fail to take the context of our texts or of our listeners seriously, we miss the truth.[40]

The expectation that theology be contextual reflects the conviction that theology taught as universally valid is inadequate. Theology is part of the search for truth and must therefore be carefully done. It ought to involve a thoroughgoing appreciation of human nature and its social, cultural, and political elements. As such, the use of contextual methods affirms an eclectic openness to the truth. In this sense contextualizing theology can be both modern and post-modern.

---

38. Contextual theologians are hardly in agreement on how and what we can learn; but the belief that we should learn is a conviction shared by all. Cf. Boff, *Theology and Praxis*, 121. Clovodis Boff argues that theological discourse and sociological discourse do not necessarily invalidate each other. He believes that the struggle over reality shared is a conflict of interpretations, which is often mutually enriching. John Milbank holds another view. He rejects the conviction that when we argue that society is a graced sphere, we give priority to social theory in our theological work. This makes a theological critique of society possible. Social concerns are essentially outside of the church and must be studied using social theory rooted in the critique of theology. Boff's approach is essentially a development of Karl Rahner's transcendental account of grace. Here a theological critique of society becomes impossible. John Milbank disagrees. For him a theological critique is the starting point. Cf. Milbank, *Theology and Social Theory*, 206ff. Both approaches are examples of the "integralist revolution" which followed upon Vatican II.

39. Käsemann, "The Beginnings of Christian Theology," 82–107.

40. Burtness, "Innovation as a Search for Probabilities," 10–13.

While liberal theologians, such as Ernst Troeltsch and James Gustafson, often accepted the social sciences uncritically, contextual theology has the opportunity to follow a critical path. Contemporary social science is following a path of integration, mirroring the need for communicative action. This is not a matter of mere coordination of terminologies or, worse yet, of coining disingenuous new ones, creating a new jargon. It is a matter of integrating different types of theories and concepts in such a way that one can formulate meaningful propositions embodying findings now sequestered in separate fields of study.[41] Theology can draw upon this model to help resource its work in a way that allows us to access contextual, scriptural, historical, traditional, and social insights within a theological process in order to ensure its integrity. The theological assessment of insights to determine their resource value is performed by people of faith, according to the rationality of faith and not that of the scientific method. As we assess the matter from our own theological standpoint of faith, we begin to do contextual theology. We cannot rush to an assessment when dealing with phenomena outside the culture text of our faith community.[42] We have to discern its effectiveness within a circle of theological reflection. Insights are represented by perspectives gained within semantic domains about the problems studied within the disciplines forming these domains—that is, the theories about particular realities (biological, political, economic, and politics).

Contextual methods focus on the interplay between the semantic domains, the conceptual and cognitive frames of reference or worldviews, the quotidian experience domains of a person's life, and the intellectual

41. Geertz, *Interpretation of Cultures*, 44.

42. Robert Schreiter in his *Constructing Local Theologies* proposes the idea of culture text as a concept that could aid us as we analyze theological communication. According to Schrieter, culture texts are unities of human communication carrying messages that can be analyzed into signs (or symbols) that carry the codes. They provide the rules by which the message is communicated. Culture texts can be as simple as a word or as complex as a nation state. Consequently, religious rituals can be understood as culture texts. All culture texts are true for those within a social group, whereas they may not be true for those that do not belong to that particular group. This truth is confirmed when the message is understood; that is, when communication occurs. When Robert Schreiter argues that all culture texts are true, what he means is that they communicate meaning through messages that everyone sharing that culture recognizes. He is not arguing for universal truth or for the acritical acceptance of local "truth". The culture text may not be true for those outside it. They may read other messages in either the sign or the code and thus misunderstand. Traditions in this sense need to be translated to ensure that they make sense. We need cultural codes to makes sense of Christian traditions.

templates that give meaning to a community's theological understanding. This is a circle of interpretation that assesses a community's beliefs and practices in terms of the insights intrinsic to its struggle to deal with the realities and find meanings in the situation they embody. It involves, from the beginning, translation and interpretation of the existential situation and life-world of people living in a particular context.[43] Contextual methods make it possible to see the context in the light of the *missio Dei*. Intercultural interpretations participate in the formation of cultural memory so that contextual methods become contextualizing theology.[44]

Bernard Lonergan, a Roman Catholic theologian, has also contributed to this discussion of cultural mediation. Lonergan studied the process, configuring the problem in the language of the social imaginary of Western Christendom. He argued that the classicist culture of the church encouraged the conviction of the "stability and immutability of doctrine." The truth of the gospel and that of Christian doctrine represent "a kernel" that can be discerned and have the same meaning in any context and at any point in history. Consequently, the issue is intercultural communication. Therefore, "primarily it is pluralism, not of doctrine, but of communications," that is at the heart of the problem. Religious pluralism acknowledges that the problem of the multiplicity of doctrine is not a metaphysical or logical problem, but one of history.[45] We cannot isolate theology from the living and changing cultural realities of the quotidian of everyday experience. The commensurability of theology depends upon inculturation. We face the problem that every context is plural and every affirmation of faith in the God of Jesus Christ is universal.[46]

Inculturation is made possible when our beliefs and practices are translated. Bernard Lonergan put it this way: the gospel can be communicated only when it is preached in accordance "with the assimilative powers of the ... culture."[47] For Lonergan the problem can be studied as the challenge of the pluralism of the means of communication. New models of theology must always take into account how a message

43. Hesselgrave and Rommen, *Contextualization*, 55.

44. Lonergan, *Doctrinal Pluralism*, 5–6.

45. Ibid., 23f., 30.

46. Ibid., 32, 53.

47. Ibid., 60.

is received and becomes meaningful for people.[48] Finding the correct concept or method is not the answer; it is rather the creation of a communicative event that is truthful. Methods are powerless. Only the Holy Spirit is powerful in this sense.

Yet ignoring method is irresponsible. We need to prepare and open our minds and hearts to the work of God in the Holy Spirit. Paul Lehmann proposed that we attend to the contextual in such a way as to preserve the interrelation between word and spirit. He said, "The dialectical interrelation between the referential and the phenomenological aspects of theological reflection correspond with the dialectical interrelation between word, faith (church), and spirit. A contextual way of doing theology presupposes and responds to a dynamic authority . . . Such a dynamic authority may be described by saying that the criteria of a contextual theology are given by the reciprocity between its method and its findings."[49] The use of contextual methods opens the way for the whole of orthodoxy in such a way as to exhibit the theological appropriateness and meaning of every formative element of the tradition, not simply of Christology, in relation to the work of the Holy Spirit among communities. It is the Holy Spirit and the openness of contextual methods that makes it possible to relate scripture and culture and free the faith community from the reign of modernity. Contextualizing theology helps the community respond to God—heart, body and spirit.

48. Ibid., 48.
49. Lehmann, "On Doing Theology," 133.

3

The Helpfulness of Theology in the Life of the Church

THE ECCLESIAL PRACTICES OF CHRISTIAN THEOLOGY

THE RISE OF THE "new Christianity" has led Christian theologians to retrieve insights within Christian traditions that are helpful as the faith takes root and forms new and vital communities and practices. According to these traditions, good theology is not a search for universal truths that can be applied in all contexts and times, but rather an engagement with the lives of peoples and communities. The eschatological framework of Christian thinking and the centrality of theological theories of God's grace ensure the openness of Christian thinking to new contexts. The creation of new Christian communities is a social and cultural process, which Christian conviction believes is possible for all and open to all. God's truth is for everyone and is not a preserve of a particular culture and worldview. Contextual theology is part of what God is doing in this world.

Central to the method of contextual theology is the conviction that theology is a response to the self-disclosing initiative of God. Theology is not revelatory, but is a response to revelation. This is why proclamation and worship are not theology, but are intrinsic to the process of theology that acknowledges the relationship between the reality of the object of our worship and the description of this reality that is constructed within the theological process within community life.

In other words, contextual methods in theology are events within the life of the church that express the openness of theology to the concreteness, the diversity, and the freedom of God's self-disclosure. Contextual theology provides the methodological assurance that the theological process is intrinsically integral to the faith community's response to its subject, the self-disclosing initiative of God.

The eclectic openness of contextual theology seeks occasions for the alignment of human knowledge and experience with the activity of God, so that the community's response can become communal praxis in the service of God. It is the formative power of the Holy Spirit that gives shape to the Christian life and in so doing provides the theological process with its material.

David Kelsey's description of theology as an ecclesial practice is helpful at this point. He draws a distinction between primary and secondary theology that I will restate here for our purposes. Primary theology, he writes, is the "self-critical dimension of every practice" of the life of Christian faith communities.[1] Primary theology is a communicative practice that takes place within the lively debate of faith communities about how to live as Christians. Secondary theology, he believes, is "inherently an analytically descriptive, critical, and revisionary practice. Going beyond description of what the traditional claims have been, it analyzes how in the past they have been used in the community's common life, how they have been understood to be related to one another conceptually and logically, what implications have been thought to be rightly inferred from them and what apparently possible implications blocked, and why."[2]

Contextual methods contribute to both primary and secondary theology within the history of the formation of Christian practice by a community of faith. They contribute to the practices of the self-critical dimension of the community of faith. The role of contextual methods is endemic to the practice of theology itself. David Kelsey defines, "Christian theology, whether primary or secondary," as "an activity that consists of enactments of a practice that is socially established by ecclesial communities as part of their common life." Contextual methodology refers to the process that establishes theological reflection at all—the social and cultural conditions that make theological life possible and the reality of the formative power of God that elicits theological response and faithful practices.

In other words, God has created a space in this world for faith communities to "do theology." This space is temporal and cultural, and as such a part of the history and narrative of peoples. The conditions are essential to the context within which God forms community. As those

---

1. Kelsey, *Eccentric Existence*, 13ff., esp. 19.
2. Ibid., 20ff., esp. 21.

who experience the self-disclosure of God, we can only respond with practices that align the knowledge we have gained from the subject of our faith with the ecclesial practices of our faith community. For them to make sense they must be communicative. Theology has always to rely upon contextual methods, if it is to take seriously the creative activity of God and the integrity of theological practice. As Paul Lehmann put it decades ago, the formative power of God "gives to the doing of theology its positivistic occasion and significance."[3]

KNOWLEDGE AND HOPE

If we accept that contextual methods in theology are intrinsic to the practice of faithful ecclesial communities, then Christian theology needs to aid communities in forming ecclesial practices that help make sense of the gospel. The place "where they/we are" provides essential resources, as well as interpretive tools for understanding the gospel. This is what the Filipino theologian, Jose de Mesa, affirms by arguing that theology is "never far from home."[4] Theology needs to think through the culture to discover linguistic and social elements that are closely interconnected, woven together with Christian understandings of God. Jose de Mesa's illustration is the Filipino concept of *loob*, or the depth of humanity. Using this interconnection, Jose de Mesa developed a doctrine of revelation that portrayed God's praxis with creation as the revelation of God's *loob* in the life of Jesus Christ. For the Filipino Christian community the use of this concept draws the listener to a deeper understanding of God that portrays the *missio Dei* as an act of graceful kindness that liberates.[5] Theology that thinks through culture and does not just translate theological doctrines captivates and inures. It helps the community open itself to the possibility of the richness of God's grace and truth.

Contextual theology is then helpful, in that it opens the minds and hearts of the faithful to the truth about God, the gospel. Christian theological practice enriches any understanding of revelation through contextualization. What is vital to a context can be put into dialogue with the full breadth of cultural insights from other cultural and social contexts.

---

3. Lehman, "On Doing Theology," 131f.

4. De Mesa, *Why Theology is Never Far From Home*, 5–12.

5. Ibid., xiv–xv.

Contextual methods are part of the theological process when the activity of the church is faithful and therefore engaged in a conversation with revelation. Only then can it become helpful as a practice of a Christian community. Helpful theology then is local and global, traditional and concrete, ecclesial and engaged in the world. Empowered by the Holy Spirit the community engages in theological work as a practice that is transformative of the Christian life.

According to our understanding of both primary and secondary theology, the practices of theology are ever about our knowledge of God. Theology is not only concerned with contextual resources; it must always be focused upon divine revelation. The text of divine revelation is the sacred text of the Christian scriptures. As a source for the theological life of communities, revelation is a special knowledge that is not analogous to our knowledge of objective and subjective realities. Knowledge of God depends upon the work of God; it is a divine gift, embraced within the narrative of a sacred book.

This is a different understanding of knowledge than that of contemporary philosophy. Such knowledge is not grasped in the same way that we intuit the solution to a mathematical equation or observe the beauty of a painting. God's self-revelation is understood as a gift that has come into the world at a particular time and place and in a concrete person, Jesus Christ. For modernity, this mystery comes as impossibility. The truth about God is not an abstract absolute, but a concrete historical and cultural particularity embedded in a sacred text, the scriptures, and the doctrines, history, and practices of the many peoples of faith. Recognizing this set of convictions is the first step in developing a healthy theology. Contextualization is not just an added extra, but is essential to the task of communicating this mystery. Contextual methods are essential in making the impossible possible and the foreign true.

In the Western centers of theological formation scholars approach the biblical text using modern biblical criticism. In the global South and among the poor, the place of the sacred text has been harbored from the waves of modern Western secular skepticism and hermeneutics. The role of the sacred text differs according to the cultural and social history of peoples. A hermeneutics of suspicion, for example, makes little sense there. This does not imply that there are advantages, but rather differences of place. Post-colonial theory has offered explanations for some of these differences, but does not offer a universal theory that explains the very core of difference in a way that is relevant for the practice of Christian theology.[6] These differences do not provide marks that distinguish the true church from the false church—the Christian from the lesser Christian. They mark differences that help define the role of contextual thinking in giving aid to communities, where they are.

Consequently, contemporary thinking concerning the nature of the social imaginary has been particularly important for contextual theology. Charles Taylor's work on secularism has been of great help as well as that of the more mainstream post-colonial and post-modern thinkers. They might offer approaches to the knowledge that concurs with that of theological and contextual methods.

This shift in the intellectual worldview of academic philosophy has been a stimulus for the development of models for contextual thinking in contemporary theology. There are two developments afoot that have contributed to this conversation and are playing a role. The first is that of post-modernity. This broad trend in philosophy discounts universalist claims concerning the nature of knowledge. The second is the trend of post-colonialism. This trend attempts to make sense of the transformation brought about by modernization and the development of "neo-colonialist" economic and political systems. Late modernist and globalized social structures are seen as the result of the rationalization of knowledge and economic systems that collude with the claim of neo-colonialist power.

The impact of the two broad trends, while frequently unsympathetic to Christian belief and the methods of theology, has stimulated recognition of the importance of the social context for all knowledge. The nineteenth century philosopher, Friedrich Nietzsche, and contemporary philosophers such as Richard Rorty and Michael Foucault, point out the vital role of social and biological context in the creation of knowledge domains and content. They show how knowledge and perspective are inseparable. Our experience shapes the insights we gain. Knowledge is produced through culture and history and not by them. This is a point that contextual methods acknowledge, although that is not the last word for the theologian. The way we shape our knowledge depends upon our experience of knowledge and power. It is given form according to the

6. Cf. Wallenstein, *The Modern World-System*; Mignolo, *Local Histories/Global Designs*. Wallenstein's work can help us understand the impact of colonialism upon local cultures.

perspectives we have gained. Arriving at insight involves conflict and it is confrontational. This has been true throughout Christian history as well as throughout human history. Yet insight is dependent as well upon theories grounded in a consensus of like-minded individuals, such as among the scientific community.[7] While post-modernity's narrow focus on conflict and power is just that, narrow, it has helped us retrieve a realistic picture of human culture and social life.

The contrast between modernity and post-modernity has been helpful for theologians who are seeking to apply contextual methods, in that they acknowledge that the modern framework is not hegemonic. Elieazar Fernandez, a Filipino theologian working in the USA, borrows insights from Foucault in constructing his theological anthropology. The new hegemonies, he argues, should be avoided, so that liberation theologies do not become oppressive through the misuse of power. Regimes of truth, he argues, can seek domination and become violent even if they are seeking to be counter-hegemonic. In other words, trying to destroy the master's house can itself become an act of hate.[8]

The "Western" understanding of truth is not meant to colonize the mind of all peoples. It was arrogant and flawed, often providing justification for racism and oppression. While modern philosophers sought to ground the nature of knowledge upon rational principles, contemporary philosophers advocated neo-pragmatism and post-modernity, seeking to portray how power and language games explain the function of knowledge. Knowledge is useful or it is powerless. Fewer philosophers are speaking of truth and falsity, reality and appearance. The problem of human nature has been replaced in some neo-pragmatists' minds by the problem of human relationships. The centrality of reason has been replaced by the centrality of self-identity. In the end, post-modern theorists argue that we are no more than bodies, whose thinking has been constituted in relation to biological and social context and environment.[9]

---

7. The deliberation over a feasible understanding of human nature has taken many turns in recent decades. The debate between Noam Chomsky and Michael Foucault as well as the stark differences between Richard Rorty and Steven Pinker reflect the divisions emerging over the problem of human nature. Cf. Chomsky and Foucault, *The Chomsky-Foucault Debate on Human Nature*; Pinker, *The Blank Slate*; Rorty, *Philosophy and Social Hope*, 117f., 126f. Foucault and Rorty emphasize socialization and social power-flows, while Chomsky and Pinker recognize something deeper in human nature.

8. Fernandez, *Reimagining the Human*, 15f.

9. Richard Rorty and other neo-pragmatists argue that this leaves no room for be-

This is, of course, too reductionist for Christian theology, but its thinking provides some help in overcoming the modernist *sackgasse*.

Critical theory has also contributed to this conversation by challenging the narrowness of neo-pragmatism with openness to social theory and rational ethical planning. This approach freed social theory to study how humans organized knowledge in order to improve and enrich human life. Its most influential advocate, Jürgen Habermas, speaks of knowledge as based upon communicative action.[10] Knowledge, so conceived, results from the interplay of power and the use of language. In this interplay what we experience as real is a social and biological construction.

As a consequence of contemporary philosophy's rejection of the narrow rationalism of modernity, the "sociology of knowledge"— founded by Karl Marx, Emile Durkheim, and Max Weber—has a new place in philosophical thinking, as it helps the philosopher to analyze social context in terms of the flow of information and expertise within concrete cultural and social settings. Both empiricism and idealism have been replaced by communicative discourse and/or the analysis of social and ideological power-flows as the question of the role of knowledge in the interplay of social and rational discourse takes center stage.

Pluralism in method is now the rule and not the exception. Knowledge is constructed within a "conflict of interpretations." Insights do not shape universally valid principles, as they might have during the modern period. Neither empirical nor hermeneutical foundations are viewed as having the last word on what is real and true. Ideologies are interpreted in terms of power-flows and communicative and cultural interactions, instead of theories grounded in methods that are modeled on foundational logic. Deductive and inductive methods of interpretation are linked together in order to shape our perspective on reality so that our understanding becomes useful.

Christian theology cannot be post-colonial or post-modern in the sense of being theology constructed using post-colonial and post-modern frameworks of thought and content. Post-modernity in its neo-pragmatist and neo-Marxist forms de-construct our pictures of reality, leaving no room for the transcendent or the numinous. There is no value

lief in God and practices based upon such belief. Rorty, *Philosophy and Social Hope*, 156–58.

10. Habermas, *Theory of Communicative Action*.

in talking about something like God as real, because nothing could be real in that sense. There is no need to recommend rational moral and scientific theories, because theories are no more than constructs, which are created by regimes of truth for their own benefit. The narrow focus of post-modernity is unacceptable for theology, in that Christian belief cannot avoid talk about God being *real* and faith being *rational*. Yet Christian theology has been aided by these reflections, because they help the theologian to do theology, in that they provide tools for disclosing cultural, historical, and social reality.

Theology that is contextually engaged is critical and traditional exactly because it is an ecclesial practice. Theology in both its primary and secondary forms is catalytic. It incites the Christian community to be authentically Christian in the context where they live. Contextual theology creates a dialogue with tradition that presses its inherited expressions to have greater integrity. Its own confessional practices are called into question and thus it introduces into the field of discussion the limits of other perspectives in understanding and insight. Theology is responsible for identifying what is genuinely human about life with God. It is challenged to express what it means to have life and communicate the truth in the world where we live. In this way theology is catalytic. Paul Lehmann, quoting T. S. Eliot, called it the "guardian of the human". As "guardian" it "refuses either to subordinate the human to its own confession or to exclude from any identification of the human, the self-disclosing initiative of the God,"[11] the creator of our context and the shaper of revelation.

CHRISTIAN WISDOM AT WORK: A THEOLOGICAL INTERPRETATION OF CULTURAL MEMORY

Another important turn in thinking is the character of the problems we now address. The awareness of the social character of knowledge carries with it recognition that the problems we raise are addressed due to social and cultural dynamics. Effective thinking should not raise questions that are not helpful. David Kelsey and Kosuke Koyama have applied this insight to their theological work.[12] They will address questions that people actually ask. Theology, like contemporary philosophy, should be clear from the beginning for whom the problem exists and what new

---

11. Lehmann, "On Doing Theology," 136.

12. Kelsey, *Eccentric Existence*, 1–3.

understanding concerning this problem can mean for those concerned.[13] Debates between scholars concerning problems that Christians do not struggle with as they seek to be faithful should not be begun.

As philosophers of liberation theology have argued though, the difference in problematic does not imply a "hermeneutics of incommunicable histories."[14] If this were true, then the suffering of the global South would leave the oppressor of the developed North untouched and in rational distance and therefore innocence. The cruelties of the world's economic reality committed throughout the modern and post-modern era would be irrelevant. This is to forget the violence of European colonial expansion. Such forgetfulness removes those who live on the periphery of the "developed nations" from sight. Is the world of the poor majority so unrelated to that of the wealthy minority that their incommensurability excludes helpful communication. The point of departure for liberation theology is that the reality of the social imagination of the wealthy can be related to that of the poor. As a result a global vision for a reconciled and humane world based upon a deeper understanding of the human condition will be possible. Liberation theology reminds us that when we discern the origin of problems we discover a critical framework for Christian responsibility. Understanding non-Eurocentric perspectives helps us to understand our own perspectives. The minimum requirement for the future of theology is the discovery of the commensurability and communicability across cultures and societies of the problems of human living and of faith.

13. This issue has been particularly important for liberation philosophers of the global South. Enrique Dussel, in speaking of the lack of "openness" and "creative capacity" among philosophers of the North, says that "the North has not paid any attention to the philosophies of the South when the former departs from its own problematics, from its own reality . . ." Dussel, *The Underside of Modernity*, 213–17, esp. 213.

14. Cf. Stackhouse, "Contextualization, Contextuality, and Contextualism," 8. In this article, Max Stackhouse rejects "contextualism" as an acritical acceptance of what is happening in a specific culture based on the argument that only those of that culture can understand it. Max Stackhouse supports the argument that there are boundary-crossing theories of justice and truth against theologians, such as Roger Haight and ethnic theologians such as Muriel Montenegro, who argue that cultural wisdom is not commensurable. Max Stackhouse argues that such theories cannot help us solve the problems of Christian theology, either global or local. They are anti-ecumenical and anti-ecclesial. Stackhouse's point against ethnic theologies is well taken.

MEMORY, PRAXIS, AND BELONGING

A valuable contribution to the study of culture has been recognition by scholars of the role of memory in social life. Paul Ricouer and Jan Assman are but two thinkers who have contributed to this discussion. Both are aware of the potential value that their work may bring to the discussion of the theological process. They begin with general observations about the social role of memory. Here are some of their insights.

All culture and society struggles with oblivion by remembering. Societies and communities labor ceaselessly to make visible, to articulate, preserve, and construct memories that struggle furiously against the disappearance and forgetfulness of meaning and identity. Culture creates markers on the road of history that prevent disintegration and stop the past from becoming meaningless. Language and other elements of culture are inseparable from the notes and content of memory itself.

The trauma of death through "disappearance" is rehearsed over and over again in Third World countries where governments practice murder against their critics. Can there be a greater threat than annihilation from the memory of ones own society? Language, politics, styles, artistic expression, and cultural developments unfold in time and space as expressions of memory. People attempt to preserve technologies of living in order to enable us to live well. Their formal consistency and guidance enable us to turn to the resources of culture to face challenges and gather wisdom for the future.

Language, culture, and political life are molded together as communities organize possible understandings of the world. They provide human beings with social reality and the capacity to imagine change. They form long-term memories and short-term memories. Long-term memories, for example, construct markers of belonging to a particular era or social group, like a family or the 60s. Short-term memories, in contrast, are reminders marking vital and not so vital moments of everyday living that affirm identity and meaning. Memory is by its very nature a confession that things change. Our expressions of memory are articulations that speed the cultural meaning of change. They hide under the cover of invisibility in the art of expressing the past. As Jan Assman put it, "the more actively the project of objectification, articulation, and notation is advanced, the more change there will be and the more forgetting." In short, the more we embody our traditions the longer they will be preserved.[15] As Jan Assman puts it, "culture is not simply a matter of memory." It constructs "techniques of preservation and principles of avoiding change that can effectively counter the tendency to vary, innovate and make accommodations. These strategies can be subsumed under the concept of 'canonization.'"[16] Culture is the way we hang on to the past. The canonization of texts is the way we shape our culture. In this way wisdom is not forgotten in the struggle against annihilation by time.

Language in written and oral forms serves the public memory of cultures as they strive for meaning. Such language makes visible authority in society, by structuring its display. Language within a Christian community, for example, is language that speaks of the past in order to prepare for the future. Public memory seeks to create monuments within our cultural space for the conveyance of wisdom and knowledge. The language of faith is such a language, when it is spoken in worship, for it fosters public memory for the purposes of the life of the community. As both Michel Foucault and Jürgen Habermas have noted, writing is an attempt to expand communication into time and space, while speech is a conveyance of lived and communicated meaning. It is not symbolically and culturally encoded so that it requires an interpreter, for if it were it would not be communication. Writing strives for the permanence of meaning and the preservation of wisdom, but it cannot ensure it. Writing is a medium of memory and not communication, and in so being aims at preserving culture so that the community can inhabit a meaning embedded environment.[17] It is writing then that makes community possible. This is reflected by the fact that in the history of humankind writing appeared at the moment in human history when social structures such as states or cities appeared. Writing is what makes it possible to inhabit communities. It is cultural memory that makes a community of faith possible. The texts that enforce this cultural memory we call the Christian scriptures. They are the canon that makes Christian belief and practices possible.

Belonging to a faith community means sharing in the historical memory of that community. The past is the resource for cultural identity and group memory. Collective memory is what makes cultural mem-

---

15. Assmann, *Religion and Cultural Memory*, 83.

16. Ibid., 84–85.

17. Ibid., 87.

ory possible. For Christians, the memory of Jesus' crucifixion or of the Exodus event binds us as a people for whom knowledge conveyed by these memories is necessary for identity. Paul Ricouer, a contemporary Christian philosopher, has discussed in detail the power of forgetting and of remembering. Memory is the capacity used in society to connect us to the cultural, political, and social resources that structure our lives.[18] He argues that literary narratives (writing) and life histories (connective memory) are "far from being mutually exclusive," they "are complementary, despite, or even because of their contrast. This dialectic reminds us that the narrative is part of life, before being exiled from life in writing; it returns to life along the multiple paths of appropriation . . . at the price of unavoidable tensions . . ."[19]

Memory is the cultural resource that binds us together. Liberation theologians such as Gustavo Gutierrez are intent on reminding us of the violence of forgetfulness, with justified reason. He argues, it is only when we remember the poor and the victims of history that the "present acquires density and substance"; and only when we remember the suffering of the past that our memory conditions us for "creative liberty."[20] When we forget those who have "disappeared," we are participating in the act of violence that separated them from the world and us.

Recollection commits us to a religious and social identity. Our social culture, its institutions and structures, exists for the purpose of creating a framework for teaching and remembering. The canonical texts that engrave the truth upon the hearts of believers are the scriptures of our faith. They provide the symbolic markers that sustain the signs of Christian identity. The biblical texts of the Christian scriptures and the narratives they share offer the literate reader and listener cultural knowledge, which becomes cultural memory, when heard as a moment of public memory.

Writing and the community form a semiotic system of cultural memory that gives stability to the traditions, beliefs, and practices of

18. Ricoeur, *Oneself as Another*, 152–63. Ricoeur's position can be contrasted with that of Nietzsche and Foucault who see memory as the will's memory, undergirding culture and community. For Nietzsche, especially, it is the will to power of the "civilizing process." For both, memory is the decisive precondition for human community and the precondition for culture.

19. Ibid., 163.

20. Gutiérrez, *Las Casas*, 457; Gutiérrez, "God's Revelation and Proclamation in History," 12.

the local church. Post-modern thinkers follow Nietzsche in regretting, what they call, the devouring spirit of cultural memory. According to Nietzsche, cultural memory subjugates and pacifies human beings according to the disciplines of modernity. Christians reject the nihilism of Nietzsche and recognize the power of memory to redeem us from destruction. In the Christian community, memory is the means for belonging to the resurrection people, the power of cultural wisdom, and the redemptive force that leads us to creative freedom and redemption. It is for this reason that the Christian community, the church, is essential for the formation of Christian identity. It is the church that offers the techniques whereby the wisdom of cultural texts can be retrieved.

The implications of these reflections for the theological process and for a theology of mission are broad and deep. Central to any understanding of the theological process, for example, must be the problems of memory and belonging. This recognition came early in the history of contextual theology. For example, Paul Lehmann noted as early as the 60s, prior to the rise of contextual theology, that the problems of theology cannot be abstract problems, which no one would ever ask about. He proposed this as the context of a reform in theological and ecumenical education. The problems should belong to those who reflect upon them. Theological problems are identifiable as they are recognized when the theologian "takes the concrete situation out of which it arises as a discipline of reflection and inquiry."[21] This recommendation was ahead of its time. Theologians are not accustomed to "listening" to the problems or questioning that arise on the periphery of their traditional problematic—that is, from the church itself. The concrete reality of the Christian community provokes theology. The practical reasoning of everyday Christian living is a provocation for theology because it gives prominence to the immediacy and concreteness of "doing theology" for the benefit of the Christian community. Theology serves the community as it seeks the integrity of its Christian praxis and practices. Theology accompanies the movement of ecclesial reflection, which "lives always in the present *out* of its past and fully *open* to the future."[22] The Christian community provokes theology as it lives with the faithful of the past and beyond them through its own witness.

---

21. Lehmann, "On Doing Theology," 132.
22. Ibid.

Authentic theology, I argue, begins by asking who is asking the questions and what is involved? Theology begins when the search for God begins among people. Theology cannot simply be resolved by discovering the preferred discussion partner. It is not set in motion by our preferences, but by God's involvement in the world. Theology begins with the grace of God. For this reason the problem of revelation has priority over all other problems for theology, not just the problems raised by contextual theology.

When we identify God at work among people, we have no choice but to begin asking questions about the meaning of God's work here with the people whom God has touched. The sources of theology are not the result of doctrine, but of faith empowered by the work of God among a particular people. In this sense theology can be scholarly, but it originates in the church. In this sense theology can never belong to a particular individual, but always belongs to a particular community.

In that theology belongs to the church, it will need to examine what this entails by raising the question of revelation. Revelation is the knowledge we gain when God is made know among us; this is something that happens because God participates in the life of peoples and individuals.

Therefore, the primary measure of good theology is its accountability to revelation, understood as theological interpretations of biblical texts read and understood as scripture. As the biblical texts are interpreted their meaning for the faithful is remembered. This is the essential distinction. The wisdom that faith communities have gained is gleaned from such theological interpretations that shape our experiences of God's presence and involvement with the world and us. Such wisdom arises as the community of faith remembers the acts of God. Experience becomes revelatory for us when it gains the status of Christian wisdom within the Christian community. It gains this status through remembering. Such authority is then rooted in the experience we have of biblical texts when they are understood to be canonical for our faith community.

The relation of faith and the life of the church is built upon the authority of scripture. The practice and process of theology critically examines its own beliefs for the purpose of shaping the common life and religious identities of the community and its individual members. Theology is enmeshed in the process by which faith communities face problems inherent in the practice of churches. It can never be disentangled. The authority of scripture is appealed to whenever practices and beliefs that are part of the life of a church are examined for their integrity and truthfulness. It is revelation, shaped by theological understanding, which helps the community preserve its integrity and remain faithful. Through practicing their beliefs in ways that are appropriate and adequate to the context of the members lives, the biblical story remains formative. This is how communities remain faithful to the mission of God in the world. It is how they remain faithful in their context.

Such theology is authentically contextual, due to the methods it uses to conduct its work. It can be articulated in a variety of modes. It can be stated in theological proposals about the way God relates to people and the world. It can be articulated as theories about how best to respond, so that the common life is properly shaped and aligned. It can recommend to the community that its response to God take forms of silence or artistic expressions that preserve an authentic and faithful common life.

Because the questions of Christian communities can never be resolved without reference to the person and work of Jesus, all theology begins with revelation in Jesus Christ, the one in whom their faith in God is based. Christian faith assumes that the knowledge of Jesus is decisive for understanding of God. Without knowledge of Jesus, it is impossible to live our faith with integrity and faithfulness. Our knowledge of God is aligned with and arises from our knowledge of Jesus, who is remembered to be God *pro nobis*.

Christian theology is not authentic, if it is not measured in terms of an adequate Christology. The person and work of Jesus is decisive for Christian practice and life. The Christian life is such, because it seeks to live responsibly in the knowledge of Jesus Christ. Its practices have integrity if they comport with the canonical scriptures and therefore appropriately witness to the God implicitly or explicitly communicated in the sharing of the biblical story. Contextual theology is one of these practices. Contextualization shapes the theology of community life in terms of an adequate Christology. This is measure of its authenticity.

In that contextual theology is a reforming practice of Christian churches, it is constructed, not in terms of particular problems, as in the loci method of scholastic theology, but according to the praxis of community living. The locus is the quotidian reality of living in community. The ecclesial practices of theology are related to how theology is taught and is constructed by the believers and theologians. It also relates to the context and the praxis of the Christian life. Systematic theology and scholastic theology can become artificial. Paul Lehmann called this the "creative iconoclasm" of theology. Doing theology prepares the community for the collapse of "its own idols," as it exhibits the idolatry of other perspectives. The activity of theology is ecclesial reformation. It participates in the life of the church with the "ongoing dynamic character of the relationship between theory and praxis." Theology arises as the church seeks integrity and faithfulness. It is not an intellectual system that prioritizes ideas and theories so that practices can be identified. The two, theory and practice, are inseparable. Clovodis Boff called their relationship a "mutual overlap that provides the possibility of both a theory of praxis and a praxis of theory."[23] Praxis informs theory in that the practices of a community of faith shape and articulate the problems. The reform that arises is due to the fact that faith informs theory. In this way the pastoral practices of a church, as well as its history, traditions, memories, and the experiences of both the theologian and the community are elements of theological reflection that always inform the theoretical part of theological work.

23. Boff, *Theology and Praxis*, 211.

4

Contextual Theology Becomes an Issue

THE EARLY SHAPING OF CONTEXTUAL THEOLOGY

A S A "NEW CHRISTIANITY" began to unhinge from dependency upon the Christian institutions of the Atlantic churches, the awareness that new ways of doing theology would emerge grew gradually and in some circles begrudgingly. In time the search for insights from Christian thinking led to engagement. Theologians such as Karl Barth, Paul Lehmann, and Visser 'T Hooft addressed the theoretical side of problems that had to be faced, such as the form an ecumenical theology can take and the relation between dogma and ethics. The key, it was believed, is found in the deceptively simple principle that faith informs theological theory to the same extent that it informs theological ethics. Significant is the timing of a letter sent by Karl Barth to Asian theologians. It is clearly intended to offer encouragement in support of creative thinking among scholars from the "new Christianity." These "Western" leaders were not revisionists or theological pluralists, but rather confessional theologians who argued for the concretization of theological work as informed by church life. They saw in the work of the "new Christianity" a chance to improve theology so that it could become what it is supposed to be. Karl Barth's involvement is representative.

In the autumn of 1969 Karl Barth wrote the last pastoral letter of his life to the "Christians of South East Asia." What he urged upon his listeners may surprise some. The editors of the *South East Asia Journal of Theology* were devoting an entire issue of the journal to the theology of Barth because they believed that their work developing theology in South East Asia would be handicapped if it ignored the "rich mine of exegetical and theological information contained in *Church Dogmatics* of Karl Barth."[1]

The South East Asia Graduate School of Theology, which had been created to develop theological education for the entire South East Asian Christian community, had just graduated its first students with the coveted Master of Theology degree. There was enthusiasm for ecumenical work and a post-colonial euphoria that was inspiring nationalist movements throughout the region.

Karl Barth did not prescribe theological premises or advise them on what to do or say. He said, "I can only encourage you . . . say that which you have to say as Christians for God's sake, responsibly and concretely with your own words and thoughts, concepts and ways! The more responsibly and concretely, the better, the more Christian!" His words contain advice that many Asian Christians have followed. With regard to being a Christian, he encouraged them to be faithful, "neither arrogantly nor faint-heartedly with regard to the religions around you and the dominant ideologies and 'realities' in your lands! Be open for all the problems which are burning in your region," and among your peoples. Be Christian, he advised, "in the freedom which is given and allowed to us and which is—according to II Cor. 3:17—where 'the Spirit of the Lord is.'"[2] We are good Christians only, he went on, "so long as we all—in openness for one another (and not to forget: at the same time also for our Roman Catholic brothers and sisters!)—belong to the one people of God, to the one Church of Jesus Christ, to the one communion in the Holy Spirit." He ended the letter with, "In the fellowship of faith, of love and of hope, I greet you all cordially as your old friend. Basel 1968, Nov 19th."[3]

I quote this letter so extensively, not because I believe that it was the catalyst for the use of contextual methods, but because Barth's comments promoted and promotes the recognition that theology needed and needs improvement. If theologians were to help the "new" faith communities of Asia and the global South they should re-think their task. Although Barth's encouragement remains to this day an abiding stimulus, he was not recommending his theology. He was calling for integrity. The call for contextual theology was not a call for new theologies with ethnic

---

1. Karl Barth, "Barth's Last Pastoral Letter," v.
2. Ibid., 5.
3. Ibid.

frameworks, but a response to the historical and contextual situation of a new era, the era of the post-colonial Third World. The call was not to be Filipino or African, but to be a *Christian* Filipino or *Christian* African in one's own context surrounded by the witnesses and suffering of one's own people and countries. The theology they developed was to be helpful in their home churches, to be useful and insightful as Christians sought to live their faith where they are. It was the leadership of the ecumenical movement, the scholarship of educators such as Shoki Coe, and the stimulus of the theologian Paul Lehmann and the biblical scholar Daniel Van Allem, who provided the scholarly framework for contextual thinking as it emerged. The success of their encouragement is reflected by the fact that contextual theologians only occasionally note their work today. They were not recommending a particular theology, but a process and a hope.

As they introduced it, contextual theology is not a type of theology; it is a response to a call for wisdom from peoples of faith and their churches. It was a call for authentic Christianity in the face of the problems of new and often very challenging contexts. A longing for reform and renewal motivated the recommendation. The call was based upon the hope that Christians could support each other, not dominate or patronize. Barth's encouragement and, we will see, the efforts of the World Council of Churches, did not call for new orthodoxies or theologies, but for a new Christianity, a better Christianity that lived according to the hope of Shalom—the hope and reconciliation in Jesus Christ. New contextualizing theology was necessary for this purpose and for the strengthening of the Christian church throughout the globe, but now according to the task at hand. It was not the Western church that was to be strengthened, but the church of Christ wherever it is found.

Stephen Bevans misleads us in his book, *Models of Contextual Theology*, when he describes the convergence of theological thinking that coalesced in a call for contextual theology as the turn to experience.[4] He argued that the call to contextual theology compels a new paradigm in theology that radically distinguishes it from all that went before. This view is far too myopic. While there may be some Christian theologians who would like to construct radically revisionist theologies divorced

---

4. Bevans, *Models of Contextual Theology*, 4. Bevans writes that, "what makes contextual theology precisely *contextual* is the recognition of the validity of another *locus theologicus*: present human experience."

from all "traditional" theologies of the past, contextual theology, as originally envisioned, is and should be conducted in continuity with the past. Contextual methods enable the committed Christian to face present challenges. It needs to rely upon the past, the language of faith of the Christian witnesses through the ages, if it is to have integrity as Christian theology. Christian theology has always been contextual in this sense, for theology has always responded to the questions of the faithful of local congregations and ecclesial communities. It may not have done this well or even consciously, but within the undertow of its very momentum it will always be drawn into the struggle to be concrete in context. In this sense contextual theology is traditional.

Stephen Bevans notes helpfully that the contextual in contemporary theology is due to a heightened and developed awareness that "reality is mediated by meaning."[5] All contemporary contextual theology studies language, memory, and culture in order to construct theologies that make sense in context. The problem of mediation is central to the debate over the quality of contextual work, as we saw earlier in the contrast between theologies that seek to mediate between the theological and the political as well as between the language of faith and that of local communities. The conflict between translation/inculturation approaches to contextual theology and liberation theologies has driven the discussion by Third World theologians from the beginning.

Theologians who identify contextual theology with revisionist trends and connect the new interest in contextual methods to the modernist philosophies of theological pluralism and liberal theologies are wrong. Such theologians as Paul Knitter, Marcus Borg of the Jesus Seminar, Alyious Pierus, Shubert Ogden, and Gordon Kaufman have promoted allied ideas; but they are off the mark. Properly used contextual methods do not promote revisionist strategies, a position that even Bevans allows. Although there are revisionists who claim that they are contextual theologians, properly used contextual methods do not promote revisionist strategies. Bevans inclusion of them goes too far here. Ecumenical theology as advocated by Faith and Order, for example, insists upon a Trinitarian framework. Revisionist theology rejects the Trinity and proposes versions of theocentric theology. What would the purpose of evangelism or mission be if the message of Christ is not the message to be shared? The original impulse actually came from strongly

5. Ibid., 4.

confessional and ecumenical scholars, such a Paul Lehmann, Karl Barth, James Burtness, and Shoki Coe. These scholars did not argue that theology is based upon the experience of a particular people. It is not like a work of art that expresses the religious identity of a particular social group or culture. The renewal they sought was one based upon the intercultural hermeneutics of context and text. The framework of Christian theology is the theological work of a global community in living out their faith in Christ. This faith is lived and practiced in the witness and reconciling discipleship of particular faith communities everywhere. Contextual methods help theology to recover and improve the process of doing theology itself. This is, at heart, an ecumenical vision, not an alternative or revisionist vision.

The ecumenical force generated by contextual methods, insists that theology remains biblical, confessional, and traditional. The experience of people matters and is essential to the work of theology, but it is not the *basis* for a theology. Experience cannot be its own justification. The basis is Christ and the goal is the formation of communities of peace, hope, and reconciliation, where people can live and witness as Christians. An ecumenical and Trinitarian orientation was evident as the World Council of Churches took up this goal in the early 70s.

Most scholars pinpoint the original impulse to "contextualize" theological and ecclesial work as a response to the expectation of the Theological Education Fund. At the time, the Fund was responsible for providing guidelines and resources for the educational programs of ecumenical institutions in "emerging" churches. They advised them to take cognizance of the context of their students and the churches they serve.[6] Theological formation and education should be connected to the everyday lives and struggles of the churches as communities. Good theology is constructed so as to mediate the gospel by becoming a part of the life, society, and culture of the faithful. They called this contextualizing

---

6. Shoki Coe, General Director of the Theological Education Fund of the World Council of Churches, and Aharon Sapsezian, an Associate Director of the Fund, developed the policies of the Third Mandate. See Aharon Sapsezian's letter in Kinsler, "Mission and Context," 24. The Fund then published two pamphlets, *Ministry in Context* and *Learning in Context*. Theological Education Fund Staff, *Ministry in Context*, 20. Also cf. Coe, "Contextualization as the Way toward Reform," 48–55; Coe, "Contextualizing Theology," 19–24. An earlier event in 1957 also focused on the concept of contextualization. That year the Rockefeller Foundation established a fund (valued at three million dollars) for "contextualizing the gospel." Cf. Schineller, *A Handbook on Inculturation*, 19.

theology, in order to emphasize its impact on the social and cultural life of congregations. It was theology in a Reformed sense of being both reformed and reforming. Shoki Coe and the Theological Education Fund are usually noted as the theological leaders who provoked the discussion leading to contextual theology. This is only partially true. There were a number of provocateurs, not to mention churches, that sensed that something needed to change, and who influenced its beginnings, but their leadership was paramount, and, I argue, dramatic.

One theologian, Paul Lehmann, a professor of Christian ethics and an ecumenist,[7] helped to catalyze the discussion in the academy at about the same time as the proposal of the Theological Education Fund and Shoki Coe. Along with Karl Barth, he may have been one of the most influential theologians to address the problem of the concretization of theology, especially among theologians of the global North. Following his path today are several theologians, such as James Cone and Douglas John Hall.[8] As noted, Paul Lehmann proposed a similar understanding of this way of doing theology in an article published several years prior to the initiative of Shoki Coe and associates. In his article, "On Doing Theology: A Contextual Possibility," he summarizes the debate over the possibility of doing theology in the face of modernity and methodological conflict. He states:

> after a century and a half of theologizing, under the worthy purpose of displacing theological speculation by painstaking adherence to the Reformer's insistence that Word and Spirit, the knowledge of faith and the experience of believing, belong together in the doing of theology, we are unclear and divided as ever about the way in which we, as theologians, are to go about our work. Consequently, we do not know how to find a way between the confessional and the scientific character of theology, between dogmatics and ethics, between kerygmatic and apologetic theology.[9]

7. Cf. Lehmann, "Willingen and Lund," 431–41. Paul Lehmann was also involved in the Lund Conference.

8. Both James Cone and Douglas John Hall use contextual methods in their theology. James Cone affirmed his commitment to contextualization early in his theological journey. Douglas John Hall argues that his theology is a North American contextual theology. Hall, *Thinking the Faith*, 69–145; Cone, "The Social Context of Theology," 17ff.

9. Lehmann, "On Doing Theology," 129–30.

His answer to the dilemma of contemporary theology was to use contextual methods in doing theology. He writes, "The method by which theology exhibits both its specific content and its positivistic occasion and significance is contextual. As a theological method, contextualism may be said to be that way of doing theology which seeks to explore and exhibit the dialectical relation between the content and the setting of theology."[10]

Paul Lehmann points to the phenomenology of Karl Barth's understanding of theological work as a good illustration. Barth's use of analogy between the Word of God and the Triunity of God rests upon his thesis that the "concrete talk about God in the church" can through the work of God as the power of the Holy Spirit become God's Word to people. He writes, "When Barth moves from the concrete talk and language about God in the church to the analogy between the word of God and the trinity of God, he is emphasizing the dialectical relation between content and setting in the doing of theology, with special stress upon what is *concretely going on* (phenomenology)."[11]

Without such a phenomenology of the concrete events of human and divine relationships, theology fails to take seriously the context within which theology is to be done. As a consequence of this failure, the distinctions between revelation and reason or theology and culture, for example, become dichotomies that cannot be overcome. When we speak God's Word, we do not have to wait for reason or cultural wisdom to speak in order for our words to become God's Word. When God's Word is heard and understood in the language of a people, then theologians are given perspective as to how to relate the content and context of Christian proclamation to the ethos of peoples posed by the reality of the human condition. The dichotomies of the modern worldview no longer place the theologian in a quandary.[12] This is a radical proposal that continues to be debated today among scholars such as Kathryn Tanner and John Milbank.

During the Reformation, he argues, "Word and Spirit referred to the self-disclosing activity of God in Jesus Christ and to the shaping of a community of faith." Apart from the "self-disclosing and shaping activ-

---

10. Ibid., 131.

11. Lehmann, "*On Doing Theology*," 131.

12. Ibid., 132.

ity" of God nothing we do in life is significant.[13] His proposal recognizes that when we focus on the dialectic of text and context we become attentive to God's activity, not ours. Our talk about the work of the church becomes concrete and connected to lived beliefs and practices. This is fundamentally an ecumenical priority.

The use of contextual methods in theology, he argues, promises to offer both the church and the theologian a way to be faithful to their tasks for the health of the Christian community. In this regard contextual theology holds great promise as a catalyst for authentic proclamation and healthy Christian community in contexts challenged by modernity. Theology's true dialogical character will be upheld, preserving the conversation between the past and the present, the pastoral theologians and the scholars, the religious and those with a negative conscience, the critics of religion.

He wrote, "A contextual theology may restore theology to its true office, which is to describe and to invite all . . . to share the power by which [we] can 'wait without idols,' and in this waiting to express [our] genuine humanity. In so doing, a contextual theology exhibits the order by which goodness is the fruit of truth and forges a creative link between confession and responsibility, between the concern for dogma and the concern about ethics."[14]

Paul Lehmann was among the first theological scholars to acknowledge the freedom from and for tradition that a contextual theology recommends. The language of the concrete life of the church is the language used by theology that can and often should be used to refer to the work of God, the *missio Dei*. Under these conditions, theology is free to take up the language of faith and thereby open up the catalytic relation between tradition and culture, so that the traditions of the church can be contextually discerned as responses to the problems of faithful living. In this way the theologian, as well as the pastor, is engaged in interpreting and translating the meaning of every "formative element" of Christian tradition. No aspect of the Christian life should be left out. The error often made by liberal and conservative churches alike has been

---

13. Ibid., 133.

14. Paul Lehmann's first version of this essay was prepared for the World Presbyterian Alliance at Hoechst/Odenwald, West Germany, in July 1965. He published an expanded edition entitled "On Doing Theology: A Contextual Possibility." Cf. Von Allmen. "The Birth of Theology," 48–49.

to make Christology the single formative element for the discernment of Christian frameworks of belief and Christian living. For contextual theology the concrete life of the community is the domain of the means for theological clarification. Christian theology must translate its language and engage the community in its response to God. Here dogmatics and ethics are perceived as "distinguishable perspectives upon a single task … the single task is the task of translating the language and conceptions of the tradition into their *human* reality and meaning."[15] The hidden premise of all contextual theology, and for all helpful and appropriate theology, is the activity and power of the Holy Spirit.

THE PROPOSAL OF THE THEOLOGICAL EDUCATION FUND

The major branches participating in ecumenical movements have embraced the use of contextual methods in mission and theology. The Roman Catholic and the evangelical churches have seen the wisdom of the proposal, as well as those associated with the World Council of Churches. The World Council evidenced their commitment through the work of the Theological Education Fund, the Roman Catholic church in response to *Ad Gentes*, and the evangelical traditions with the efforts of the Lausanne Committee for World Evangelization. The ecumenical movement laid the groundwork, but the hard work has been carried on in all three. Within the evangelical community, the Lausanne meeting of 1974 introduced contextualization largely in relation to methods of evangelism, but also as a framework for embracing issues of social justice. A few years later in 1978, a journal of the *Partnership in Mission*, entitled *Gospel in Context* began publication. Since then evangelicals have been seriously engaged in both their scholarly and mission work with the problem of contextualization. In the Philippines, for example, a constant stream of publications and regular conferences dealing with contextualization has ensued.

To gain our bearings, let us look first at the work of the World Council of Churches that led to the introduction of contextual theology. The Second and Third Mandates of the Theological Education Fund set the stage. As James H. Berquist has shown, the history of this process is best understood in "relationship to the pilgrimage made by ecumenical

---

15. Lehmann, "On Doing Theology," 134.

mission theology . . . It was its task or mandate to assist the formation of theological education in Third World countries. As colonialism came to a close after the Second World War, the Theological Education Fund was directed to provide guidance for churches caught in the ferment and upheaval of their times. They were faced with trying to find a way to live life as Christians in a rapidly transforming world. The fire of change was becoming a testing ground. The Theological Education Fund was launched in 1957–58 in Ghana. This led to the First Mandate (1958–64), which was to encourage academic training as the means for the formation of church leaders throughout the Third World.[16]

The goal was to form an academic infrastructure that would sustain quality church leadership. It emphasized the development of faculty, improvement of libraries, and the basic educational training of church leaders. Reflection began upon the means for aligning these goals with indigenous education models.

The Second Mandate of the Theological Education Fund (1965–70) was to serve exactly this goal. It recommended the kind of theological education that should be encouraged among the "younger churches." The Mandate acknowledged the need to rethink theological education based upon ecumenical understanding and a missiology helpful to churches trying to face the cultural and historical realities of Asia, Africa, and Latin America. So conceived, theological education was "that kind of theological training which leads to a real encounter between the student and the gospel in terms of his own forms of thought and culture, and to a living dialogue between the church and its environment."[17] In other words, theological training was to prepare church leaders who would empower transformative change among the peoples of the Third World. The change envisioned included theological and ecclesial change, as well as a newly formed participation in social and political change. It was an authentic response to the Uppsala Assembly of the World Council of Church held in 1968 that emphasized renewal in mission. The ultimate goal of mission is not the establishment of ecclesial institutions, but Shalom, which "involves the ultimate reconciliation and unity" of all creation "in Christ."[18]

16. Cf. Coe, "In Search of Renewal in Theological Education," 234.

17. Theological Education Fund, *Ministry in Context*, 13.

18. World Council of Churches, Uppsala Assembly. Second Section, *Drafts for Sections*, 34.

The economic domination of the West continued just as former colonies strove for independence. To exacerbate the problem, the economic leaders of the former colonies perpetuated dependence for their own advantage, furthering the dominance of the wealthy and powerful. In addition the lure of the West coincided with one of the greatest changes in human history, marked by the unique drama of the 1960s and its counter-cultural "discovery" of the self and the lure of Western prosperity and life-style.

The drama of the 1960s precipitated a transformation of the cultural and political landscapes of virtually every nation on the planet. The shifts in thinking and living were accompanied by a re-threading of the social fabric to the extent that the social imagination of virtually every nation on the globe has changed. These shifts often are subsumed under the category of secularization, although this may be too simple.[19]

The new ethos can be described as the ethic of authenticity and it took shape in the decades after WWII and came of age in the general culture in the 70s. Combined with the dramatic increase in the "quality of life" which this new imaginary presented to the world as possible, the lure of the West became almost unbearable. Be Western and you can be yourself, a wealthy self with all kinds of technological wonders at your disposal. Challenged by an alluring Western cultural dominance, the Theological Education Fund issued a Third Mandate (1970–77). It addressed in more concrete terms than before the threat of the secular ethos that promised so much, just out of the reach of the people of the Third World, and which displaced faith in the lives of "successful" people.

The Third Mandate called upon theological education to offer help for those who were searching for meaning in this new secularizing context, to confront the social injustice built into the impact of neo-capitalism and the corruption it imposes, and to empower local cultures to face the marginalization that accompanies technological advances.[20]

This was the hinge that allowed the theologians of the Third World to open the door to the promise of contextual theology. It also marked a significant shift in the ecumenical movement's understanding of mis-

19. Taylor, *A Secular Age*, 473ff. He writes, "I believe, along with many others, that our North Atlantic civilization has been undergoing a cultural revolution in recent decades. The 60s proved perhaps the hinge moment, at least symbolically" (ibid., 474).

20. Cf. *Ministry in Context*, 13.

sion. After this turning point it was impossible to speak of evangelism isolated from the problems of social justice and liberation.

Shoki Coe states that it was during the debate over the future of theological education that the concepts "contextuality" and "contextualization" arose.[21] He writes that they were convinced that the "interaction between text and context" guides the process of theological formation. Funding from the TEF was to promote contextualizing theology for the purpose of embedding the interaction of text and context in the theological and ecclesial lives of local churches.[22] Theological formation should address issues of justice, align with local culture, encourage a healthy theological process, and produce a "servant ministry." These expectations remain intact to this day. Seminaries of theological formation throughout the Third World continue to evaluate their work according to these criteria, even when they are not aware of their origin.

While proposals for the form of contextual theology have abounded, the term contextual theology has yet to settle into a common discourse. Nonetheless the original definition of contextuality by Shoki Coe preserves the sense of the problem that we continue to struggle with today. He says contextuality is the "critical assessment of what makes the context really significant in the light of the *missio Dei*."

The goal is to face the challenges of the era, currently understood to be the era of secularism and oppression, and enable churches to discern where God is at work so that the faithful can join God at work. The goal is to participate in the *missio Dei*. While there are many approaches that seek to respond to this goal, often in direct conflict, those theologies that

---

21. Shoki Coe argued, years later, that contextualization is the most serious task of the church in that it is the means by which the church reforms itself. It is the concretization of the principle of *ecclesia semper reformanda*. The preferred term for the process of reform at the time was not contextual theology but rather "contextualizing theology." Contextualization, Shoki Coe, argued is not a simple acclimatization of theology, but rather the creation of a new context through the encounter of a people of faith with the Word of God. It is a spiritual event within the church that empowers transformation. Cf. Coe, "Contextualiztion as the Way Toward Reform," 49–50. Some scholars have taken this to mean that the TEF recommended contextuality—the characteristic of being attentive, conditioned, rooted, shaped, and inclusively focused on context. The original intention of the TEF, however, was to use contextual methods so that the church, its mission and its reality would be embedded in the context. For this reason, I focus in this book on contextual methods and not contextuality. Cf. De Mesa, "Being Mindful of Context: Characterizing 'Contextual Theology.'"

22. *Ministry in Context*, 31.

welcome the name of "contextual" agree on this summary. It is for this reason that "contextual" theologies require social analysis in order to understand the pernicious, liberative, and ambiguous aspects of modernity and secularism. They also need hermeneutical models for interpreting the role of Christian tradition in the face of cultural diversity and stress. The argument was deceptively simple; as Christians grow in awareness of their historical and social environments, they become better able to respond authentically as Christians.

Pluralism in theology has made it impossible for the neologism "contextual theology" to have a precise definition. Nonetheless the use of "contextual theology" to describe what theologians are doing marks an openness to focus on the problems of modernity, secularism, and tradition for the global church, not just for the churches of the Atlantic societies.

The debate has often centered on the contrast between liberation theology and evangelical theology. This has been an unhelpful and shallow debate. Among some the debate has been forced into the choice between theological pluralism and confessional theology. This contrast has distorted the issues from the beginning. The goal of contextual theology is to improve the theological process in the face of the development of a global church. If the political, economic, and cultural realities of the Third World were to change dramatically that would not mean that contextual theology should be abandoned. It is not tied to certain contexts or even political and economic solutions to the historical realities of the Third World. It is tied to the enrichment of all Christian communities, wherever they may be found, not for their own purposes but according to the purposes of God.

Contextual theology is ecumenical theology exactly in its orientation to mission understood as *missio Dei* and therefore as mission which has as its goal, the Shalom of God. It is as such confessional and not ethnic. It is not theology that seeks to promote a particular denomination, but theology that empowers the confessional tradition of belief in Christ within a particular context. It is not theology of a particular people, but theology for particular peoples that empowers each person and each community to participate fully as part of the body of Christ. Contextual theology does the impossible in joining God creating Shalom.

Consequently, theology that partitions peoples according to confession, race, or ethnicity fails to understand the theological task. God does not propose to raise up one people over others to dominate and control them. God is creating the kingdom of God through the sending of his Son and his disciples into the world for the sake of its salvation.

Assumed in the basic strategy of contextual theology is that the questions of theology should be answered as responses to particular situations, but the answers do not arise isolated within these situations alone. While contextual theology is local theology, it is not assumed that this is Christian theology simply adapted to a particular situation. Rather it is an interpretation of Christian living and believing in a particular context. Interpretations of the meaning of Christ for faithful living can be and are often meaningful beyond the particularity of the local theology that gave it birth. Contextual theology brings the constant study of the Bible and the constant study of the situation of living in a particular context together and engages them in a conversation.

Lesslie Newbigin wrote these words at the end of his life in appreciation of the new turn in ecumenical thinking. He said, "Every communication of the gospel is already culturally conditioned. The word 'contextualization' seeks to . . . direct attention to the need so as to communicate the gospel that it speaks God's word to the total context in which people are now living . . ."[23] He adds, "contextualization accords to the gospel . . . its power to penetrate every culture and to speak within each culture . . . the word which is both no and yes, both judgment and grace."[24]

RESPONSE TO THE PROPOSAL

First, let us look the Roman Catholic response as one development illustrating the reception of contextual theology within an ecclesial domain. The Roman Catholic Church throughout the world took steps to contextualize mission and pastoral care on a global scale. At the Second Federation of Asian Bishops' Conference held in Calcutta in 1978, for example, the plenary assembly sought to address and clarify what is implied by inculturation. The result is found in articles 10 and 11 of their final statement. Inculturation was discussed in terms of the values and commitments of the Roman Catholic tradition.[25]

23. Newbigin, *The Gospel*, 142.

24. Ibid., 152.

25. The complete Final Statement of *FABC II* is found in *FABC Documents*, 27–48. By "values," the FABC is referring to "spiritual values" such as "the discipline of ascetics,

Article 10 argues that inculturation is the means for handing on tradition. Necessary is the "creative assimilation and "translation" into contemporary cultural expression." Inculturation is part of the pastoral process to renew Christian "communities within contemporary society." Contextual methods realize "'spaces of silence and worship' in the lives of believing men and women." Article 11 argues that this "creative labor" implies that pastoral work "must assume into the full Christian life of our peoples what is good, noble and living in our cultures and traditions— and thus in our hearts and minds."[26]

The understanding of inculturation taught by the FABC argues that contextual methodology not only translates the content of Christian belief so that it becomes meaningful, it also integrates what is "good, noble and living in our cultures and traditions." Similarly Paul Lehmann had proposed a dialectical relation between gospel and culture, content and setting. What is new is the explicit recognition that the language of faith of Christian communities includes pre-Christian cultural elements that can and ought to be assumed as authentic witness to the work of God in the world. The FABC acknowledges that this dialectical dialogue of critique and enrichment is essential for healthy inculturation. The model proposed acknowledged that the intercultural interpretation of gospel and culture, context, and text was part of the concrete reality of Christian communities. We borrow and transform the cultural elements of our context for the purposes of communicating the gospel.

The FABC spoke of this as integration. The Holy Spirit is the author of integration in that it is the Spirit that leads as the community forges the Christian tradition anew from the resources of culture. Integration translates the Christian beliefs and practices according to the purposes of God and thereby embeds Christian tradition within the cultural, spiritual, and social world of the community of faith. Such praxis is holy learning that is good and enriching. Here theology is done for the good

---

a deep and innate religious sense, filial piety and attachment to the family, the primacy of things of the spirit, an unrelenting search for God and hunger for the super-natural" in *FABC II*, article 7, in *FABC Documents*, 30. According to the *FABC*, the current situation of Asian Christianity threatens precisely those values that form their tradition. Cf. *FABC 1*, arts. 4–6, 18–19; *FABC II*, article 8, in *FABC Documents*, 30.

26. *FABC Documents*, 31. Here they refer to Second Vatican Council, *Ad Gentes*, 18. The language, throughout, resembles that of Vatican II and French theological and ecumenical thought.

of the church and of the *missio Dei*. The Bishops spoke of a "fuller catholicity made possible in this age of the Church."[27]

In order to study how to promote a "fuller catholicity" the International Congress on Mission was convened in Manila in December 1979. The Second Consensus Report of this Congress is entitled "Local Asian Churches and the Tasks of Mission: Inculturation".[28] The report argues, as a counter to its critics, that inculturation is not adaption to culture but "a creative embodiment of the Word in the local church." This is the basic and fundamental method for contextualization advocated by the Congress. Almost echoing the proposal of Paul Lehmann they argue for "a dialogical encounter process," perceived as participation in the "salvific movement of the Triune God."[29] In this salvific moment evangelization occurs as "a dialogue between the gospel message and the given reality . . . conducted in humility and mutual support" seeking "the fullness of Christ." They buttress this interpretation by a reference to *Ad Gentes*. Article 8 reads, "The mutual exchange of their discoveries among the local churches will lead to their enrichment as well as that of the universal Church." In this way the church and the culture are redeemed, healed, and reconciled to God by the power of the Holy Spirit.[30]

The FABC's proposal for inculturation as a dialogical process of mutual enrichment is a concrete means for facilitating a theological process within the life of a local congregation. In order to facilitate the dialogue as a catalyst for a healthy theological process within the church, the laity should be encouraged to read and understand the Bible and study the traditions of their church, so that a deeper spirituality may evolve. In this way theology is not just an abstract analysis of beliefs, but an integral element of the shaping of peoples lives according to the purposes of God.

It is interesting to note the priority the Report places on "festivals and community celebrations." The events are not to be discouraged, but rather transformed through intercultural interpretation. Perceptions of the practices are to be altered so that the social imaginary that gives

27. *FABC II*, article 31 in *FABC Documents*, 35.

28. *CPW II* in *FABC Documents*, 138–41.

29. *FABC I*, 12.

30. *FABC Documents*, 138–39.

these events meaning is reformed and "healed" as they are "interpreted in the light of faith."[31]

The importance of this document, and others like it, for the Roman Catholic Church cannot be overestimated. The centrality of incultura-tion marks a turn towards contextual methods in Roman Catholic prac-tice and theology. This turn is aligned with the Second Vatican Council's advocacy of a new direction in theology, which they hope will lead to the transformation of ecclesiology. The church is no longer perceived as the church of Christendom but as a missionary church. As *Ad Gentes* stated it, "The church on earth is by its very nature missionary since, according to the plan of the Father, it has its origin in the mission of the Son and Holy Spirit."[32]

A contextual theology of mission places missionary activity at the heart of the church's faith and life—not as an appendage. Roman Catholic mission theology has explored Vatican II's contextual directives and Trinitarian framework. Within this strategy, the deepened aware-ness of the role of the Holy Spirit is contributing to a contextual theology of mission with implications that are appreciated across confessional divides.[33] The theology of evangelism, as conceived according to contex-tual methods, is inseparable from pneumatology, linking missiology and ecclesiology to a recognition of the Holy Spirit as the principal agent of evangelization.[34] These are significant improvements in Christian theol-ogy, which are helpful for ecumenical understanding and the enrich-ment of world Christianity.

Optimism about the promise of contextual theologies must be coated with the bitter recognition that often little generosity is shown by well-established Roman Catholic churches toward the use of contextual methods by non-Western churches. Nonetheless, there are a number of churches that have taken the new direction to heart. For example, in the Philippines where scholars and pastors have welcomed the use of con-textual methods, the church itself shows change. In the Catholic Bishops

---

31. Ibid., 140–41.

32. Second Vatican Council, *Ad Gentes*, 2; cf. Second Vatican Council, *Lumen Gentium*, 1.

33. Cf. Bevans, *Models of Contextual Theology*; Costa, ed. *One Faith, Many Cultures*; Metz and Schillebeeckx, eds. *World Catechism or Inculturation?*; Shorter, *Toward A Theology of Inculturation*.

34. Paul VI, Apostolic Exhortation, *Evangelii Nuntiandi*, 75.

Conference of the Philippines held in 1999 in preparation for the new millennium, there is evidence of a role for contextual methods. A reference to the success of the new Catechism for Filipino Catholics, which is referred to as "inculturated and authentically Filipino," is representative. Inculturation here is translation. Later, however, the Archbishop Oscar Cruz, President of the CBCP wrote a pastoral exhortation devoted to inculturation. While the motive to use contextual methods in the life of the church is often weak in spite of the new developments within theological formation and the theology of mission and evangelism, concrete steps are being taken.[35] We see them in Protestant, Roman Catholic, and evangelical churches.

As noted earlier, these developments within Roman Catholic missiology and ecclesiology are matched by comparable changes in the theology and praxis of established Protestant and evangelical churches. Mission today necessarily is understood within a new recognition of the value of contextual methods for ecclesiology promoted by the World Council of Churches, Vatican II, and the Lausanne Committee. What has emerged is a new vision of Christian mission, a new openness to the modern world, and a spirit of reconciliation and renewal. The work of the church is no longer conceived in denominational or secular terms, but as the work of the Holy Spirit inspiring God's redemption of the world. These changes can be seen as manifestations of the Holy Spirit, reconciling and redeeming the world according to God's purposes not ours.

More specifically, the turn to contextual theology enabled Christian theologians to seek new approaches and new forms of evangelization, and to discern the Spirit's presence within secular movements and events. Intercultural interpretation of the world's realities is no longer something just useful for the church; it is necessary, because God participates in the struggles of people. Struggles against injustice manifest human dignity; thus, mission demands that Christians see that the Spirit of God is present bringing hope and life within these developments as the poor and oppressed suffer. The Spirit is present, and immanent, preserving and giving life, in the face of human destructiveness and evil. Mission leads to contextual discernment of the social, political, economic, cultural, and religious "signs of the times," for the sake of God's purposes in the world.

---

35. Cruz, "Pastoral Exhortation on Philippine Culture," 194ff.

This vision of the Spirit's presence within the world is foundational to the use of contextual methods.[36] In Asia, for example, this is often called "doing critical pastoral-theological reflection." Such methods take for granted that Christian theology concerns God's word for humanity. Consequently, the human in all its concrete social, political, ethnic, and political reality, that is the *humanum* with essential dignity as a creature of God, is a partner in the dialogue between gospel and culture.[37]

Approaching theology in this fashion means beginning with "what is going on in human society and the world," with local cultural realities and values, with the traditions and aspirations of people. In short, the world and human reality "set the agenda" for this approach; yet tradition and scripture are never excluded. They are essential to contextual methods because they inform the theological process in the construction of both primary and secondary theology. Using the insights of David Kelsey on the work of primary and secondary theology, we can see how this takes place. Primary theology, as the theology of self-criticism, takes place as ecclesial communities reflect upon whether their beliefs and practices are appropriate to their understanding of God. It studies appropriateness, quality of concrete praxis, and the perspicuity of these beliefs and practices. Contextual theology helps at each stage as the ecclesial community examines the language and witness to their faith. Primary theology is concerned with received traditions, doctrines, practices, and perspectives on reality. Secondary theology is the practice of ecclesial theology that proposes more adequate traditions and doctrines, based upon insights and questions raised as the community seeks to live out its life according to the help provided by primary theology.[38] Both activities within the life of ecclesial communities require contextual methods in that the problems of appropriateness, perspicuity, and normativity are solved through cultural insight and the quality of communicative praxis.

Mission theology today engages theological and pastoral contextual method, because through it local theologies evolve under the Spirit's guidance. These theologies develop within ecclesial communities as Christians prayerfully reflect in the light of revelation on events, move-

---

36. The central point of John Paul II's Encyclical Letter, *Redemptoris Missio*, states that the Holy Spirit is the principal agent of mission. See *Redemptoris Missio*, 21–30.

37. Kelsey, *Eccentric Existence*, 190ff.

38. Ibid., 17ff.

ments, and realities of the local and global church. In this manner, the entire church is enriched with faithful theologies as she listens to the Holy Spirit.

Let us now focus on a few central points of this discussion. When the idea of contextual theology entered into the missiological debate during the early 1970's in documents emanating from the World Council of Churches in Geneva, Switzerland, it was proposed as an improvement on the concept of "indigenization" in theological education, which was common then and remains prevalent today. Its meaning today has been deepened by including it within the more complex and responsive framework of contextual theology. Indigenization was often understood according to the metaphor of the seed planted in soil. So conceived, indigenization was too weak a concept for understanding the relationship between gospel and culture. The confrontation between gospel and culture was interpreted as applying an abstract and transcendental gospel to an intractable and alien traditional culture. The gospel could never be fully embedded and at home where it was no more than an exotic plant in a controlled greenhouse.[39]

Contextualization was considered a more appropriate concept for the dynamic process they sought, because contexts are indigenous and transformable. According to the proponents of contextual theology it is the text of the gospel that is the catalyst and transformative element of the creative encounter of gospel and culture. Otherwise contextual theology is a flawed version of situational thinking. In situational reflection the gospel is a product of the situation alone, defined by it and evaluated in its terms. In contextual theology, the gospel brings something novel, redemptive, and reconciling that is formed in the culture with this encounter. The text-context paradigm informs the contribution that contextual methods make to the theological process. Scriptural interpretation makes intercultural interpretation possible. We find this represented in both Protestant and Roman Catholic approaches to contextual theology.

In South Africa, for example, the terms contextualization, contextual theology, and contextualization of the gospel are used primarily to describe the process of relating the gospel (the canonical text) and the community's response to the gospel (text) within the realities of Christian living (context). Many South African contextual theologians,

39. Niles, "Towards a Framework of Doing Theology in Asia," 16–28.

for example, are Protestant, so the principle *sola scriptura* is advocated from the beginning as the essential resource for theological reflection. The relationship between the scriptures and their context in the life of people is predominant. Yet, as we observed earlier, we find this to be prevalent among Roman Catholic contextual theologians as well. Asian Bishops were insistent on the centrality of scripture even in the process of assuming new practices of Asian cultures not present in Christian cultures.

The text-context framework for understanding the viability of theological work only breaks down as theologies are configured as ethnic theologies, which propose that the community itself is the text which, when illumined by the light of religious faith (scripture) confirms the community's experience as the primary resource. Ethnic theologies are unpersuasive because they identify divine revelation with a community's experience. The experience of liberation from one tyrant could become just a new experience of oppression. This does not mean the loss of Christian hope. Our hope does not lie with a political or ethnic achievement. It lies with Christ. For example, many liberation theologies have argued that the poor were taking their own histories into their own hands and joining liberation movements. If the poor do not join these movements, they are not lost and without hope. Christian beliefs and practices are not illegitimate if we fail to overcome evil.

The South African missiologist David Bosch understood the value of this framework. He refers to the new theologies of mission as advocating an "emerging ecumenical paradigm."[40] New contextual and ecumenical methods change the way we construct theologies of mission and evangelism. By stressing the need to manifest the inter-relatedness of all the different ways in which God's mission is accomplished, the differences between denominations and cultural and ethnic division are diminished and the barrier to God's work is permeated and removed.

The success of this ecumenical paradigm of mission and theology is the recognition that it has made it possible for theologians to do their job well. As Lesslie Newbigin put it, "True contextualization accords to the gospel its rightful primacy, its power to penetrate every culture and to speak within each culture."[41]

---

40. Bosch, *Transforming Mission*, 368ff. and 457ff.

41. Newbigin, *The Gospel in a Pluralistic Society*, 152.

Contextual theology is often associated with the dramatic changes that have led to the transformation of Christianity in the global South, and the religious pluralism of this "new Christianity." The ecumenical vision of unity and diversity that has motivated ecumenical and missional movements within Protestant, Catholic, and evangelical churches has been encouraged by the recognition that Christianity need not be tied to any particular culture or worldview. The one church can and does come alive in multiple cultural, social, and religious contexts. Theology can aid the church to exhibit visible unity in the transformed world; in fact it should.

The rise of the "new Christianity" does not mean that Western theological scholarship no longer can contribute to the theological life and ecclesial formation of the new churches. While the critique may ring true that Western theology has been "on the side of the privileged," it is not the theology of the West that is invalidated. It is the failure of its social and political ethics to take seriously the poor that is rejected. The weakness of Western theology is that it did not study the situation "within which the theologizing communities were immersed." Western theology "just did not address them and in ignoring them let injustice go unquestioned."[42] The dilemma that permitted this to happen was the artificial separation of ethics from dogmatics. Contextual methods, as Paul Lehmann and Shoki Coe proposed, are intended to overcome this separation so that theology can be what it is supposed to be by doing what it is called to do and be.

It was the introduction of contextual methods that permitted Christian theology to take steps to overcome the failure of the West to confront injustice. Liberation theology, for example, introduced social analysis that interpreted context in terms of the economic, ideological, and cultural reality of poverty.[43] Context here refers to the social context discerned from an analysis of the quotidian perspective. Liberation theologies have differed significantly as to how to analyze and identify the quotidian perspective but the conviction that social analysis is vital is held by all versions.[44] There have also been differences in opinion as to the boundaries of legitimacy. Robert Schreiter, for example, has at times

42. Kalilombe, "Third World Theologies," 1–2, 6; Kalilombe, *Doing Theology at the Grassroots*, 150; Gichure, *Contextual Theology*, 80ff.

43. Segundo, *An Evolutionary Approach to Jesus of Nazareth*, 21.

44. Haight, *Alternative Vision*, 18, 26.

been accused of arguing that all theologies are local and therefore their insights cannot be shared across cultural borders.[45] His semiotic method for studying the potential of contextual theologies has given the false impression that the use of contextual methods would lead to an infinite number of local theologies hermetically isolated from each other. This is certainly not true. He is clear that insights can and ought to be shared across cultural boundaries for the enrichment of everyone and the formation of a new catholicity.[46] Robert Schreiter rebuts the argument. He writes, "One must posit a certain commensurability of cultures, in the sense that all cultures may receive the Word of God and be able in some measure to communicate with one another . . . [or] give up either the universality of salvation given by God in Jesus Christ or the fundamental unity of humankind."[47] He is argument is simple and elegant.

If this is so, why are we not celebrating our unity? Much has yet to occur in order to live out the true catholicity of Christian churches. We are not graceful in our relations to those who are different. Why has there been so little generosity toward the application of contextual methods up to now among scholars and ecclesial hierarchies of the churches that advocate for it. Efforts to inculturate and apply contextual methods are vital for the new Christianity that is at our door. We need to take seriously the role of theological thinking in the formation of Christian identities among the new congregations and faithful communities throughout the globe, not just in our backyard. We need to accept the gift of unity in Christ that God through the Holy Spirit is forging among us.

In short, we should recognize that all theology is local and contextual with global reach and contact. Traditional Western theologies are also the result of the creative work of the church in encounter with culture. The text-context pattern of theological work that elicits praxis, reflection and intercultural interpretation is found throughout Christian history and is the nexus whereby the church becomes an agent in the history of peoples and communities.[48]

We conclude as well that all helpful theology at this point in history is also liberative. Given the state of the world, the church cannot avoid

45. Schreiter, *Constructing Local Theologies*. Cf. Kraft, *Christianity and Culture*, 291ff.

46. Schreiter, *The New Catholicity*.

47. Ibid., 128f.

48. Soskice, "The Truth Looks Different from Here," 43ff.

the responsibility to share the good news in contexts where liberation from injustice and oppression is essential for the communication and concretization of the gospel. Damage to human life is now a global experience, as is our share in responsibility for the damage that predominates. Our context makes clear where the challenge to faith lies. The challenge is not grounded in weak "secular" arguments about the existence of God, but in finding ways to confront suffering and evil.

Contextual methods determine the nature of the damage and the depth of the suffering. Therefore they can uncover before the church the possibility and path of liberation. Through biblical and spiritual discernment, contextual theology is capable of offering help to congregations and communities. Thereby it can detail the nature of Christian responsibility before such evils as racism, sexism, consumerism, abuse of human rights, decaying global and local environment, and economic crisis. Contextual methods are essential for every theological theory, especially those that acknowledge the centrality of the *missio Dei* in defining the nature of the church, in that their use confirms the inseparability of the universality of salvation and the unity of humankind.

Speaking in response to Barth's theological approach, Paul Lehmann said, "When systematic theology learns to be less ambivalent about its own positivistic character and more sensitive to a contextual way of doing its work, it will know how to deal at one and the same time with its own content and setting and with the ethos and the options posed by the human situation in which systematic theology must work."[49] It seems that he was right.

---

49. Lehmann, "Doing Contextual Theology," 132.

5

Sources and Processes

Contextual Theology and the Emergence of a Christian Community

PROCESS OF HEALTHY CONTEXTUALIZATION:
THE CIRCLE OF CHRISTIAN THEOLOGY

A N ARGUMENT OF THIS book is that the proper theological use of contextual methods is healthy and promotes and enriches the life of faith among Christians around the globe. As the theological process is enriched by contextual methods, the community is enriched and empowered to greater service of God in Christ. This is a claim that needs to be illustrated and defended. In this chapter, I will attempt to examine this thesis.

By recalling here a biblical story, I believe that I can demonstrate a contention of contextual theology that the biblical text is the catalyst for the formation of Christian community and the theological process. This will support the aim of showing how healthy the use of contextual methods can be. Telling a central biblical story should show how the cultural memory embedded in the text leads to a re-rooting of its meaning in a new context. The story I will recall is the story of the road to Emmaus, which can illustrate how a biblical and theological interpretation of a central biblical story can make an ecclesial event possible. We can see how the Christian life is a life in a faith community.

Contextual reflection is unavoidable when the Christian community gathers in faith, for it is in this movement that identity and service are rooted. To be Christian involves, from the start, a journey begun in faith that leads us to ask what it means to be Christian in the place where one lives and where the community seeks to live out the mission

that God has prepared. This simple narrative framework follows a logic
that includes contextual reflection by necessity. For the early Christian
communities this journey was accompanied by stories and parables that
prompted and channeled the theological process. The formation and
preservation of Christian beliefs and practices are inseparable from the
telling and hearing of the Gospel. Through listening to these canonical
stories and texts the journey forms faith and life. Today the doctrines
and traditions formed throughout the history of Christian living must
be dusted off and reformed along the same path as before. The Christian
story does not have a lifecycle like a plant or animal. It is not born, only
to die. It lives on as the story is told and the journey that God has prepared for the people of God continues.

Perhaps the Emmaus story in Luke's Gospel is one of the best biblical texts for illustrating how the Christian life leads to faith seeking
understanding.[1] The narrative relates the beginning of the Christian

1. Luke 24:13–35. "Now on that same day two of them were going to a village called
Emmaus, about seven miles from Jerusalem, and talking with each other about all these
things that had happened. While they were talking and discussing, Jesus himself came
near and went with them, but their eyes were kept from recognizing him. And he said
to them, 'What are you discussing with each other while you walk along?' They stood
still, looking sad. The one of them, who name was Cleopas, answered him, 'Are you the
only stranger in Jerusalem who does not know the things that have taken place there
in these days?' He asked them, 'What things?' They replied, 'The things about Jesus of
Nazareth,' who was a prophet mighty in deed and word before God and all the people,
and how our chief priests and leaders handed him over to be condemned to death and
crucified him. But we had hoped that he was the one to redeem Israel. Yes, and besides
all this, it is now the third day since these things took place. Moreover, some women of
our group astounded us. They were at the tomb early this morning, and when they did
not find his body there, they came back and told us that they had indeed seen a vision
of angels who said that he was alive. Some of those who were with us went to the tomb
and found it just as the women had said; but they did not see him.' The he said to them,
'Oh foolish you are, and how slow of heart to believe all that the prophets have declared!
Was it not necessary that the Messiah should suffer these things and then enter into
his glory?' Then beginning with Moses and all the prophets, he interpreted to them the
things about himself in the Scriptures.

As they came near the village to which they were going, he walked ahead as if he
were going on. But they urged him strongly, saying, 'Stay with us, because it is almost
evening and the day is now nearly over.' So he went in to stay with them. When he was
at the table with them, he took bread, blessed and broke it, and gave it to them. Then
their eyes were opened, and they recognized him; and he vanished from their sight.
They said to each other, 'Were not our hearts burning within us while he was talking to
us on the road, while he was opening the Scriptures to us?' That same hour they got up
and returned to Jerusalem; and they found the eleven and their companions gathered
together. They were saying, 'The Lord has risen indeed, and appeared to Simon! Then

movement as Jesus himself revealed the truth about himself to his followers as they journeyed to Emmaus. As such, it is a good resource for explaining the theological process, due to its role in connecting our journeys to Jesus' path as faith is instilled. The main narrative elements of the Emmaus story coincide with steps taken within an ecclesial event as believers listen to the gospel and enter the Christian life. They culminate in the ecumenical sacrament, the Lord's Supper or Eucharist. As Jesus traveled with them, they talked and saw things anew as communicative action transformed their situation.

As disciples of Jesus we are on a journey sharing their struggles. As they talked Jesus joined them. In an ecclesial event Jesus joins us and listens. He does not let us alone. Yet without listening to him we cannot know him or the truth about our situation. He is not recognizable to us until we hear him speak.

He enters into our lives by talking with us as God's Word. When disciples gather communicative action results due to the presence of Jesus. Dialogue concerning the events of their lives within their world narrates the drama of the story. As they were talking with each other, Jesus became part of the conversation. One of the necessary characteristics of an ecclesial event is that faithful believers gather and listen to the gospel. One of the essential beliefs of the Christian community is that when we gather, Jesus listens to us.

Another Christian conviction evident in the narrative is the belief that even when Jesus is present with us we need help to recognize him and to understand what he is saying. When he "comes near" he is not recognizable for who he is. Because of who he is and who we are, limited human beings, we do not recognize him. Our understanding is limited by our human nature. Like the disciples on the road to Emmaus our eyes are "kept from recognizing him." We need a story, a revelation, to know who we are and who Jesus is. This is the human situation. We need the text in order to make sense of our context. Revelation adds something that is not simply a consequence of the history of our lives. Our journey becomes an kairotic event when Jesus changes everything because we recognize him in the midst of the world and our lives. Jesus is the mystery of the world and we do not see this until we recognize him.

---

they told what happened on the road, and how he had been made known to them in the breaking of the bread.'" (NRSV)

Jesus cares about us and our struggles, so he has them share them. It is as they share and interpret their context that they see the world anew. They recognize him at the table. They do not understand until they hear the biblical story and they do not recognize him until he interprets the biblical story for them and shows himself as the one who sat at their table at Jerusalem. The presence of Jesus changes things in that through him the Holy Spirit opens a new vision of the truth. Because of the text we can see how the events of human history fit into the story of God. Through hearing and listening, the *missio Dei* is unveiled. The story of the work of God with the people of faith and for the world is made known.

Because he "interpreted to them the things about himself in the Scriptures," they could understand. Through this experience of the resurrected Jesus Christ and the hearing of the gospel, they experience and see the world differently. Their faith is renewed and they begin to follow Christ and witness to the good news. Mission and evangelism become possible. The result of the event is that faith seeks understanding and mission. A theological process emerges as we remember who we are and who God is. Contextual methods are necessary in order to complete the steps in a healthy, engaging, and faithful way.

A simple pattern is repeated in Christian history every time the faith is shared, the Word of God is heard and Christ's presence at the table is experienced. This is the narrative structure of the theology of Christian worship, mission, and evangelism that brings text and context into action. In this key story for the foundation of Christian living we see mirrored the beginning of the Christian life. We cannot make sense of this story, if we cannot picture who we are before Jesus, or what God is doing. Contextual methods make the connection between our lives and the life of Christ visible for us. This is what contextual methods provide. The transcendent cannot be known without a world where the drama is being realized. The message cannot make sense.

As they arrived, he walked on as if he was heading somewhere else, but they needed him so that their faith and knowledge could grow deeper. It is only when he breaks bread with them that they recognize him and their faith is in him. They see things anew and become Christians. This is the pathway that leads to the formation of Christian identity. It is the pathway, the story, of discipleship. Paul Tillich spoke of such moments as *kairos* moments, when the kingdom of God breaks into our time.

When seeing things anew, our understanding no longer impedes faith, and conversion—in both moral and spiritual terms—happens. We turn our lives in the right direction. This story is impressed with the structure of an ecclesial event. We believe and become disciples, when we see that the kingdom is at hand through Jesus.[2] Faith and commitment coincide when recognition happens; and recognition can only occur when understandable language and cultural forms are used to communicate the reality shared as the gospel. Recalling and recognizing who Jesus was reminded them who they were. Once they knew who they were, because they knew who Jesus is, they returned to Jerusalem. This leads to the next step. They acted on their faith.

For this reason, both the interpretation of Christian scriptures and contextual methods are of immense importance for all Christian theology. They provide the boundaries of the domain for all theological theory.[3] Theory within the theological process is theory about God's revelation, and the relation of biblical text and our context. Because the theological process is motivated by faith seeking understanding and an authentic life with Christ, a doctrine of revelation and canonical scriptures is essential. Therefore, theological theory is constructed upon the central relevance of Christian scripture for our knowledge of God.[4] Practice within Christian theology is the practice of witness, in that the insight we gain compels us to live according to God's purposes. Theology is motivated by the desire to understand God and the proclamation of the wisdom we gain in the event of revelation. It is constantly renewed as the worshipping and serving community gleans new insight while listening to the gospel being proclaimed. Communicating the story in words and events that make sense to people is essential.

In short, this is what motivates the Christian community to reflect theologically: the story of God and of the people of faith. When Christians profess their faith, they confess that this story is their story. They discover that it is the story of ultimate importance in their life as faithful human beings. Within the story of God, who is revealed through listening, they confront the God of Israel and discover this God at work

---

2. Mark 1:15.

3. Ritschl, *The Logic of Theology*, 68–72. Cf. first chapter of Matheny, *Theology of Christian Churches*, 7ff. I discuss the positions advocated in this section of this book in more detail in the first chapter of Ritschl, *Theology of Christian Churches*.

4. Oracion, *Human Realizations of Grace*, 35ff.

within the life and work of Jesus Christ and his disciples. As they find God in scripture, they find God at work in their lives today and confess God's presence in the lives of those witnesses who have gone before them. In this way, Christian scripture is constantly the source of new insights into God and of renewal within the life of the Christian community. It is the context that offers us the possibility of configuring the insights for the spiritual health of the community. Because God is understood anew, this is the source of continuity and discontinuity within the Christian community. It is also its source for its vitality and conviction. Helpful theology participates in this renewal. Without the use of contextual methods that render the story of God in ways that clarify the reality of our lives before God, the renewal does not happen. We cannot recognize God.

To have faith in the God of the Christian scriptures is to trust the God of Jesus Christ. The Christian community affirms that God is trustworthy. One of the basic beliefs of faithful Christians is that faith itself brings us into a right relationship with God. This insight is often spoken of in terms of the principle *soli fidei,* which states that the right relationship to God is based upon faith alone. Belief instills an attitude of openness to the reality of God and divine grace. The insight gained is received *soli fidei,* that is, due to the revelation received through faith in the reality of God. Through the Spirit and a helpful rendering of the story, the reality of God breaks through and grants us awareness.

Through faith, Christians put their lives in perspective. Through faith, they perceive reality and the truth about God and themselves. Faith determines the truthfulness of one's entire existence. If Christian faith is true, a Christian may live a life near to God—the God who determines all existence. If our faith is bad, we are on the wrong path in life. This is true for communities and institutions as well as for individuals. It is true for all life in general. Through the relation between tradition and scripture, contextually connected, life is redeemed. In Asia and the Third World, awareness that the relation between contextualizing theology and authentic living is growing.[5] Hopefully this awareness will spread.

The subject matter of witness, and consequently of our search for understanding, is the reality that faith opens to us when we trust in God. This reality is the self-revelation of God or God's story with people. This story illustrates how faith instills a relationship with God. When God is revealed to us in the Christian scriptures, we find a new reality opening

5. See for example the essay by Jose, "The Future of Filipino Theology," 255–69.

to us. We develop a perspective on reality that is true, and consequently sensible and fruitful.

When we trust and believe in God, we affirm our faith in the faithful One, who makes divine faithfulness known to us. God's story is a story of self-revelation. God becomes known to us. We do not grasp who God is; God grasps us. We cannot investigate the reality of God in the same way we would investigate an objective phenomenon. We can only open ourselves to God's graceful presence as we worship, listen, and live. Contextual theology assumes that our relationship with God is not substantive or material in nature, but relational and personal. Faith establishes a relationship that opens all of reality and the truth about God the Creator and Redeemer to us. Many theologians have argued that because theology begins *soli fidei* the basic attitude of all theology should be the attitude of prayer. Theologians assume the attitude of openness practiced by Christians. Christians practice in worship and prayer an *ascesis* or technique of the self that opens the heart and mind of the Christian for the work of the Holy Spirit.[6] It is this technique of self that recognizes the priority of God's self in the relationship that matters for Christian theology—the relationship of encounter with God that is the prerequisite for all events that communicate the truth about God in Christ. These events are rightly called ecclesial. This is the relationship of faith. For theologians who believe theology is performed in an attitude of prayer, theology is faith seeking understanding.[7]

To affirm Christian tradition is to retrieve the biblical and classical Christian traditions, which confess that God speaks to us through the Christian scriptures.[8] These traditions belong to all Christian move-

---

6. *Ascesis*, in this sense, is not the asceticism of early Christianity, but the turn away from self that recovers the self in relation to God. God is the actor in the event of revelation that occurs through this *ascesis*, which is the fundamental form of spirituality for the Christian. Such a turn does not achieve self-knowledge, but knowledge of God through the work of the Spirit in the prayer life of a faithful person. It creates an openness of the self to the help offered by God.

7. The classical text illustrating this conviction is Anselm of Canterbury, *Cur Deus Homo*. Contextual theologians have taken this approach. Examples of such theologians are Gutierrez, *The God of Life*, xiiii–vii; De Mesa and Wostyn, *Doing Theology*, 127–29; and Oracion, *Realizations of Grace*, 36f. The Latin phrase to designate this recognition is *Fides Quaerens Intellectum*. Calvin put it this way: "*omnis recta cogntitio Dei ab obedientia nascitur.*" Theology that begins from this perspective begins with faith and the knowledge of God.

8. Scripture references such as Ps 19:7–8; Matt 5:18; Rom 3:2, 12; 2 Tim 3:15 have played an important role in Christian piety reinforcing this belief for Christians.

ments today and in the past. For both Calvin and Aquinas, for example, it is God's presence in our lives as we hear the Word that is central to our understanding of God, not the literal word itself.[9] The Spirit is not limited to the text, but rather the Spirit is among us and with us, inviting us to believe and have faith. Most contemporary theology, since Karl Barth, has sought to retrieve and renew this approach. Although there are some critics—who continue to use a scholastic or process model— that disagree, theologians today are returning to the source of scripture and to the aid of theological interpretation and contextual methods as ways to conduct their work in and for the church.

According to this model, scripture is our canon because it is the witness to the fullness of time, the time when God was with us in Jesus Christ.[10] Because the fullness of time occurred at a certain time and place, we must take its history very seriously. Jesus lived in a world that was both Semitic and Hellenistic. For the gospel to be shared in the first centuries of the Christian movement, it needed to be "translated" from the cultural and linguistic forms of the world of Jerusalem into the broader culture of the Hellenism of the Roman and Persian worlds. The good news needed to be stated in communicatively viable forms. It was this uniquely Hellenized version that reached the entire world.[11] The vernacular thought forms of Jesus' time were the medium in which the message was proclaimed.[12] Time was full only then, so we should turn to this history, the language of witness during Jesus' life, and the way of thinking of his disciples and potential followers, for insight into God's Word for us today.

Consequently, in order to use contextual methods well, we need to learn to think within a biblical framework. This framework is a prerequisite for interpreting and communicating God's story, so that it can be heard and understood today. It is the Bible and the invitation of the Holy Spirit that opens our hearts and minds to the "strange new world" of the story of God. This is so because we come to realize, through proclama-

9. Plantinga, *Warranted Christian Belief*, 241–46. To account for our knowledge of God we need, according to the Calvin/Aquinas model, scripture, the invitation of the Holy Spirit and faith in God.

10. See my discussion on canonization earlier in this book. Here I am referring to the classical definition of canon used in traditional theology. They are related.

11. Cf. Sanneh, *Translating the Message*; Walls, *The Missionary Movement in Christian History*.

12. Sanneh, *Translating the Message*, 56–61; Bosch, *Transforming Mission*, 447–48.

tion, who God is and whose we are. The story of the road to Emmaus illustrates this paradigm. We will not know how to use our language until we know Jesus' language concerning God. True communication stands and falls here.

From its earliest days, Christianity has struggled intensely with the determination of what we believe, why we believe it and the basis of our belief. This is no different today in the churches of the "new Christianity" from those of the first century. Each community raises these issues anew, as the context and challenges change. New questions arise that need to be addressed, because Christians are seeking to be faithful and live out their lives with integrity according to the demands of their context. Christian thinking is contextual in ways that other religious thinking is not. The Christian message is lost without contextualization.

One reason that this is so is that each era and context has its own questions and problems, language and cultural reality. As each new generation seeks to articulate its beliefs, it discovers that its knowledge of faith grants new insights. New challenges and historical situations call for new responses and new knowledge. Christians seek to respond to their world in words as well as in action. Faith seeks understanding as an inspired quest for the truth for the people we serve and the peoples God touches.

For each community, a theological process is initiated which will retrieve and develop biblical traditions of the church that have become so hardened or forgotten as to repress and forget the faith inspired by God's story with us. These debates and confrontations have informed Christians throughout the world and throughout the history of Christianity. Each issue has had a significant impact upon what we believe and the way we live our faith. It has enriched and at times congested the theological process.

Just as early Christians sought to preserve the integrity of their witness and faith in Jesus Christ, contemporary theologians are proposing guidelines that, in addition to those of early periods, may be helpful in our cultural, social, and historical context. There are conditions today that mark our era as unique. Now that Christianity is global and not characterized by the struggles over empire of ancient to modern times, as it has been since the first centuries of Christian history, we are rethinking both our confessional traditions and what it might mean to re-tradition the new movements of Christians arising throughout the world.[13] Contextualizing theology makes this renewal possible.

During the Reformation era, for example, the guidelines of *sola scriptura*, of the centrality of proclamation and of the priesthood of all believers, were applied in order to reform the beliefs of medieval Europe according to biblical wisdom. To do this the eschatological framework was restored to its proper role, so that the Word of God could once again be proclaimed authentically within the life of the Christian community. Using contextual methods that communicated the biblical story in a way that made sense to people and retrieved Christian traditions necessary for renewal, reform was sought. Both Protestantism and Roman Catholicism were re-formed in the wake of the retrieval and restoration of eschatological thinking. Today we need to think how this and similar retrievals may be accomplished for the churches of the "new Christianity."

In the churches of the "new Christianity" of the global South, there are new problems, such as the impact of globalization and the "prosperity" theology of many Christians throughout the world. One of the problems that has occupied both theologians of the 70s and those of today is poverty. In my classes I engage my students in a conversation about poverty and the way it may impact the theological process by introducing the theological process proposed by Gustavo Gutierrez, one of the molders of Latin American liberation theology. At the beginning of the 90s he proposed a method for theological reflection that demonstrates the importance of the contextual in the theological process.

While theologians of the Europe and the North struggle over skepticism in the face of modern doubt and bias, he argues, theologians of the impoverished South raise the issue of theodicy, in the face of the poverty that dominates their lives. In response, he recommends a direction informed by hope to live as Christians in a context dominated by devastating poverty. While not everyone can or should agree with his proposal, any theologian doing theology today should not forget the

---

13. Jenkins, *The Next Christendom*; Sanneh and Carpenter, eds, *The Changing Face of Christianity*. In Joel Carpenter's preface of *The Changing Face of Christianity*, page vii, we read, "In 1900, 80 percent of the world's professing Christians were European or North American. Today, 60 percent of professing Christians live in the global South and East . . . Today, Christianity is a global faith, but one that is more vigorous and vibrant in the global South than among the world's richer and more powerful regions."

face of poverty. For this reason, I believe, his approach is notable and challenging.

Let us look at this proposal before we continue to discuss the theological process. His proposal suggests a pattern of questioning that is related to the history and social and cultural context of the theologian. As such it offers a valuable illustration of how the use of contextual methods informs the theological process. I will condense his proposal for our purposes.[14] According to Gutierrez, the context sets the agenda. We live in a time of doubt created by greed, anxiety, and skepticism, so the questions cannot be isolated from the suffering of believers.

As Christians living in the Third World, he says, we do not ask the question, "Does God exist?" in the same way as a scholar at a Western academic institution. In the Third World the issue that pervades peoples' lives is not doubt about whether God exists, but that God exists. Among the impoverished of the Third World, this question is not raised in doubt, but becomes instead an affirmation that God exists. The poor are the faithful poor, for whom God is very much alive. The poor share with the biblical witnesses the firm conviction that their God is the source of our very being and the giver of life.

Consequently, Christians in the Third World do not find the philosophical God of the classic Western tradition convincing. The God who gives life is not an abstract God, an unmoved mover or a principle. The God of their faith is the God they know from scripture—a compassionate God; the God they know loves. They believe that God cares enough to free them of the burdens of oppression and death. When they worship God, they learn how to see the world and each other through God's eyes. The God of the poor is the God of life, the creator, redeemer, and sustainer of the world.

In that the poor do not experience God as abstract and distant, as the deist might, the only way that they experience the divine is through *koinonia*. God's word and our witness prepare the ground for truthful experience of God. The God we discover is none other than the God of the biblical story. God is in the kingdom that Jesus proclaims, the

14. Gutierrez, *The God of Life*, xi–viii. Gutierrez raised these questions as a contextualizing method for acknowledging an understanding of the God of the Bible. His intent was to open up a perspective meaningful for people of the Third World. His argument that the poor have a right to articulate their own theology is compelling. I discuss this in greater detail in my *Theology of Christian Churches*, 13ff. This illustration is repeated here from my lecture notes for my class on the introduction to theology.

kingdom of God. The God of the poor cannot be the God proclaimed by the oppressor. God's kingdom is not made concrete by the progress of a particular civilization, economic system, nation, or political party. The kingdom of God is the kingdom of justice and Shalom. It exists wherever Jesus is Lord and God's people live according to God's purposes.

They know God because they have experienced God among the faithful poor as they worship and witness to the kingdom. They can talk of their suffering and their God, because they believe what they have heard and seen as they share and listen to God's words for them. They know because they have experienced the Holy Spirit working among them. They experience the God of the biblical story and of the kingdom of Jesus and seek to align their lives according to the purposes of the ever-present giver of life. Their lives are lived in anticipation of the help God offers and the hope that the Holy Spirit awakes.

Yet they experience their situation as one of tension and conflict. How can a loving God allow such oppression, hunger, and death? Contextualizing theology among the poor must begin here, with theodicy. For this is the fundamental challenge of their lives. Their lives must become a living answer to this question. Because they know the God of the Christian scriptures, they know that God is setting things right. Their vision and mission is born in the faith of the believer; so that the world will be set right and embraced in the life of God and not doomed to the emptiness of death. The faithful poor know that God is at work redeeming the world and that they can participate in this ultimate transformation.

In a world of death and suffering, this pattern of theological reflection can help the theologian keep their language of faith, concepts, beliefs, and practices focused on the gospel. While this pattern may not be applicable to all contexts around the world, it is hard to argue against its value or authenticity. We are each called to reflect upon our context in order to promote a healthy theological process in our local churches, as means to preserve authentic and healthy communities of faith. Our response will promote contextualizing theology and is a necessary element in preserving and forming vital Christian beliefs and practices. Our future as Christians depends upon our integrity as theologians.

Contextualizing theology that has discovered the God of love leads to worshiping and faithful community. It is not a theology based upon a theological pluralism or even a broad inclusivism. Faith leads believers to be engaged in the transformation of society and of peoples, from a perspective committed to the uniqueness of Christ and the God of life.[15] Pastors, laity, and scholars are all theologians.

This leads us to a final point about the theological process. When Christians seek to live faithfully, they must proclaim responsibility and witness authentically. Consequently, the relation of responsible proclamation and faithful witness must be clear.[16] What guidelines are there for helping us to understand this relationship? Contemporary theologians have used metaphors to describe the movement of this relation. One is the circle and the other a dance. In doing so, they are arguing that a fruitful theological framework is based upon circular thinking that allows the dance of responsible proclamation to be authenticated by witness in the world.

For example, we learn from the Emmaus story that our lives and beliefs are faithful when we know Christ. The first thing we learn, when we listen to this story, is that our lives are valuable in God's eyes. Jesus is concerned about the events of our lives. He is to be found in them, listening to us. Secondly, our ability to see and understand is limited by human nature. We need to be given sight by Jesus. Social and cultural reality needs illumination from beyond its resources. Human culture does not provide the resources for truth. We need to be open to transcendent realities for wisdom. We need cultural media and events in order to point to the transcendent. The many ways of seeing can hamper or aid us in this. Seeing may be recounting the events to others and between us. Jesus encourages us to recount them and he listens as we do. Seeing becomes perceiving. Contextual methods deepen insight and strengthen meaning as they make things intelligible. Jesus opens our eyes so that we see. Our story relates to the events of his life. Our journey joins the spiritual journey of the people of God. As we reflect on this text and context in the light of the gospel, our faith and commitment are given shape. Judgments about what goes on in our lives are illumined by the life of Christ. Our insight is inspired by the *kairos* moment; our belief and practices are authenticated. The search for knowledge links our life

15. Boff, "Epistemology and Method of the Theology of Liberation," 20–21.

16. Edward Schillebeeckx in support of this belief wrote, contextualization issues in "a proclamation which will on the one hand remain faithful to the word of God and on the other hand will allow that word to ring out in a way which does not by-pass the reality of this life." Schillebeeckx, *God the Future of Man*, 3.

to the events of Jesus' life and thereby to the life of the people of God. We are all walking the path prepared by God. We study the scriptures in order to interpret our world and follow Jesus. Through ecclesial events we experience *kairos* moments, and our lives are redeemed from the shallowness of *chronos*—ordinary time. Finally this story becomes the gospel, inspiring commitment to action and praxis. The Emmaus story, in our example, is a powerful metaphor for the Christian life.

Shoki Coe's insightful emphasis on the contextualizing nature of theology is helpful at this point. A healthy theological process leads to a contextual church. Such a process recognizes and encourages the "right to think" of Third World churches, so long repressed by Western dominance. Liberation theologians such as Clodovis Boff argue that this movement concretizes theology, both primary and secondary.[17] Even if one does not accept the overall project of liberation theology, his point is well taken.

As is clear here, contextual theology becomes an element of the theological process whenever the question of what it means as an individual or a community to live in Christ is raised. Good theology is healthy for the community. It provides the Christian community with essential tests and measures for the authenticity and health of its theological process. In this way contextual theology is an essential part of the faithfulness of an individual and of a community of faith. It participates in the construction and formation of a faith community's ecclesiology. In envisioning a lived and critical insight into the truth of the gospel of Jesus Christ, it empowers a particular church to follow Christ. It is this particularity that spells out Christian responsibility.

Christian theology, when it is responsible contextualizing theology, initiates critical reflection upon the quotidian point of a particular human being and the faith community of believers. The context of a particular faithful person is always the locus of contextual theology, in that it leads to the theological circle. Within the theological circle, the domain of the theological process is circumscribed and the place where theology is formed and re-formed is given shape.

---

17. Clodovis Boff sees this as the challenge by the secular to the sacred. For him, secondary theology is the theology that addresses the problems of culture, secularity, history, politics, etc. Like other liberation theologians, the connection of secondary theology to the practices and beliefs of the church is left undeveloped. Boff, *Theology and Praxis*, xxviii ff.

The work of contextual theology is not complete unless it considers as well the relationships between the theologies that are part of the overall formation of a faith community's theological process. Movements of contextual theology align with the theological process of faith communities. Like a dance the two perspectives move back and forth, learning from each other and posing the questions that contribute to the formation of healthy theology. To perform this dance we need to take two steps. First we need discern the quotidian reality. We need to be aware of the multi-dimensional reality of the lives of particular human beings and their community of faith before we can understand how to reflect upon this existence. And, second, we need to identify the transforming insight and Christian wisdom that follows from faith in the gospel of Jesus Christ. Having performed this dance, we can align our lives according to the purposes of God in Jesus Christ.

In order to begin to align our lives properly, we need to take at least two more steps. These steps will lead to the formation of a contextual ecclesiology. Contextualizing theology issues in an ecclesiology that is both indigenous and faithful. Because by using such methods the theological process connects the history of a particular people with their part in the overall Christian story. Finally the hope of unity within diversity can be concretized. In this movement an awareness of the inter-ecclesial context grows, whereby the reality and mission of a particular church is related to that of other churches and the overall history of Christian communities from the beginning of the Christian movement.

Contextualizing theology leads to responsible theology. Contextualization is what happens when a religion becomes culturally embedded. Contextualization is the creator of our problems as well as the means for addressing them. Unhealthy contextualization leads to unhealthy faith communities. The theological process is suppressed and the biblical story distorted. Yet, it is a process that continues as long as the faith of the community is vital. It will happen when the Word of God is heard among people of faith. The work of the Holy Spirit makes visible God's vision for that community and helps the faithful to be clear about their mission as God's people. However, the loss of vision will lead to the loss of a clear sense of mission.

As noted the proposal to contextualize arose as a response to the urging of the World Council of Churches to reform theological education. The renewal called for was summed up on the Third Mandate. At the heart of the Third Mandate was a theology of the *missio Dei* that emphasized praxis. Contextualization is more than an effort to embed Christian beliefs and concepts within culture. It leads to participation in the mission of God where God is at work redeeming, liberating, and reconciling the world. Christian contextualization is an element of the work of the Church.

At that moment in the history of the ecumenical movement, ecumenical leaders turned to the theology and example of Dietrich Bonhoeffer to talk about the true and confessing church. Through contextualization a Christian community could participate fully in the world according to the cause of God. As Bonhoeffer emphasized, the church should not serve itself, but others. The mission of the church is the mission of God and therefore the work of the church should be liberative and reconciling. The church is the instrument of reconciliation and liberation and therefore the continuation of Christ's work in the world. Reconciliation means being reconciled to God and to neighbor (the world). Shalom is peace where justice and reconciliation are total. God is at work in the world reconciling the world. This is the true force of the movements of history. The church then should be a catalyst for liberation and reconciliation.

Contextualization, in this sense, is not simply a method for conversion. It is a part of the historical process of the mission of God. It is essentially the participation of the faithful in the struggle of peoples for Shalom. Shokie Coe speaks of the interaction of contextuality and contextualization. It is this interaction that is the focus of a theory of contextual theology. Theology must be reconfigured so that the separation of the academy and the church is overcome. It is a call for integrity that calls for all theological theory to align with Christian praxis.[18]

Theology can no longer be inattentive to the struggles and misery of the peoples of the world. The motive for contextualization was the awareness that theological conviction was not embedded healthily in the lives of many around the world. The connection between beliefs and the peoples' lives had become weak. Beliefs shaped by scholastic theological theories were removed from the concrete struggles of people. Such theology had become a copy of the belief systems of earlier contextualized theology, removed from context. The Christian theology, both of the oppressor and the oppressed, had become so abstract that their beliefs were

18. Coe, *Ministry in Context*, 24.

robbed of their prophetic and reconciling power. Truth had become the repetition of orthodox propositions; it was no longer lived and empowered by the Holy Spirit. Consequently, the church needs renewal through contextualization.

Shoki Coe recognizes that this involves an invigorated engagement with the Bible. Shoki Coe and James Burtness reflect the influence of Karl Barth by speaking of the biblical texts as "mere earthen vessels" that point to the transcendent reality of God. The responsible theologian is required to interpret the biblical texts anew so that Christian theology may be re-formed to respond to the *missio Dei*. James Burtness insists that we are to re-contextualize the text.[19] Our illustration of the Emmaus story shows how this could be done. Given the circle of theological thinking, every effort to interpret the text is therefore an event of cross-cultural communication.

At the same time, we should not forget that there are dangers in the contextualization process. Theological reform is itself a part of the theological process. It can harden into doctrine that convinces so well that it resists contextualization when its time comes. Yet, it is contextualizing theology that makes it possible for theology to do what it is supposed to do. It can only do this with humility before God and what God is doing and will do in history. As Edward Schillebeeckx reminds us, our efforts are "only one small voice within a great movement which began with Christ and the apostolic church with its Scripture and has continued throughout the ages. Every part of this great historical process is therefore at the same time a criticism of the tendency to make another part of this tradition absolute."[20] In his work, Lamin Sanneh has documented this process with its hardening and elasticity. He argues that cultural assimilation leads to the hardening of theological positions and practices so that Christianity may seem exportable in total. This happened as the early Christianity became culturally captive within a Hellenized world.[21] Yet it is through mission that cultural captivity is challenged and dethroned. Christianity can and does migrate, but primarily according to the vernacular principle, which leads to inculturation. We can see the damage this has done to mission and evangelism by the fact that

---

19. Burtness, "To Re-contextualize the Text," 13.

20. Cf. Schillebeeckx's "Foreword," in Schoof, *Breakthrough*, 2.

21. Sanneh, *Translating the Message*, 56ff. It is through mission that the cultural captivity of Hellenized Christianity was challenged.

in many countries around the world, European Christianity is identified with Christianity *per se*. The illusive lure that a particular version of Christianity can be universally applied everywhere in all times and places has been attractive to both traditional Christians and critics of Christianity, as they advocate a modern understanding of the nature of cultural orthodoxy.

Paul Lehmann recognized this problem and offered a solution. To address this problem we need to recognize, "that traditional theological language (confessional, liturgical, doctrinal) has a referential as well as a functional significance. Whether this language is retained or abandoned depends upon the referential clarity and power with which this language functions." We need to discern the place of traditions in the process by which the faith becomes at home among a particular people. When we are discerning, "the formative elements of orthodoxy function as conceptual instruments of theological clarification."[22] They aid the proclamation of God's Word and do not hinder it. Here the beliefs and practices of Christian faith are not pictured as exportable doctrine. Through healthy inculturation, orthodoxy becomes reformed in the alignment of Christian beliefs and ethics according to the purposes of God. Doctrine is not simply the norm of faith but has become the "instrument by which what faith knows may be interpreted and communicated."[23]

ECCLESIAL TRADITIONING AS A CULTURAL REALITY

The practices and beliefs of Christian communities are not imported, but rather faithful works of the people of God prompted by the Holy Spirit. For example, the practice of the public reading of the Bible assumes the work of the Spirit; otherwise listening to Christian scripture is not worship. It is this that shapes the proclamation, the beliefs, witness, practices, and praxis of Christian churches. The work of the Spirit forms community and calls it into being. It empowers the church with truth, purpose, and direction. The Roman Catholic theologian, Avery Dulles, has helped us to understand this process by providing us a helpful analysis of the importance of scripture in local church life.[24] He reminds us

22. Lehmann, "Doing Theology," 134.

23. Ibid., 122.

24. Dulles, *Models of Revelation*, 209. Speaking of the Christian Bible Dulles says, "it is an instrument in the hands of God, who addresses his church by means of it. The Bible forms the consciousness of its own readers, brings its own horizon with it,

that the existing church community was responsible for the scripture. From what we have seen in the process of contextualizing theology, we can say that the statement of responsibility can be reversed: scripture is responsible for the existence of the community.

The shape of the biblical narrative was formed by the faith of a community in order to provide a witness to Christian faith that could be shared and lived. Apart from the community of faith, there are no Christian scriptures. The Bible is composed of a story of peoples who sought to make sense of the God of their faith. Their desire to know was always exhausted by the limitations of their own understanding and experience. Their understanding grew as the Holy Spirit worked among them.

We can draw several conclusions here. First, the Christian scriptures are limited by the understanding of the faith communities of the past. They are the final written deposit of a process of traditioning that incorporates written and oral traditions concerning the story of God with people of faith. It was only in the community of faith that these materials were collected and became authoritative. Here they become fundamental elements of a community's cultural memory. They were guided by the Holy Spirit and concerned with the future of the community as an authentic witness to the events that gave it shape. They collected materials that interpreted these events for listeners in their world and that taught the nature of the authentic praxis of life within a faithful community of believers.

The process of theological interpretation takes seriously the conviction that the Christian scriptures contain compositions of individuals and peoples over time and in their own world. It also takes seriously the reality of the involvement of the Holy Spirit with particular people living in a unique context. In addition, the entire process is understood as the work of the Holy Spirit and of the community of faithful. The result is a canon that the faithful trust and believe is authoritative for all Christian churches. When the story of God within the canon is proclaimed the church becomes the church through living the Christian life. Preparing

---

and thereby shapes a tradition of interpretation. The Christian reader, dwelling within that tradition, will allow the Bible to establish its own framework of meaning, forming, reforming, and transforming its own readers. The Bible's proved capacity to enlarge and stabilize the vision of those who submit to its power is one of the reasons why it has come to be accepted as inspired."

the way for this to happen with integrity is the responsibility of Christian theology and the ministers of the gospel. Contextual methods insure integrity.

The Christian scriptures and the embedded traditions of Christian churches work together with the Holy Spirit to form and transform the life and beliefs of communities of believers and through them of the peoples of the world. The Scottish Presbyterian theologian, Thomas F. Torrance, has pointed out that the traditions of the church in the form of ecclesial dogmas are "fluid axioms" that are formed, re-formed, enriched, and retrieved in the light of revelation.[25] They become structures through which the truth can be revealed in new and perhaps unsettling ways. We are, like the ancient readers of the biblical story, engaged in the same process of traditioning that enriches our experience and knowledge of God. While we experience the proclamation of the church differently from those whose witness is recorded in scripture, each of us is engaged in the interpretive task of forming a deeper knowledge of God. We are engaged after the Christian scriptures have become our book; they were engaged, as the texts became scripture. The goal is for their sermon to become ours, as far as it proclaims the truth about God in a new and very different context.

It is the primary activity of proclaiming the gospel that constitutes the community of faith. The ecclesial event of gathering as a faithful community and listening to God is the truth-bearing event giving form to the Christian community and its spiritual life. Christian scriptures and traditions are inseparable in the event of proclamation through the work of the Holy Spirit, when text and context are dialectically related. This is the core process of the theological life of Christian communities. Consequently, scripture, tradition and the living and proclaiming community of faith are all results of the work of Christ in the world for the sake of the reconciliation of the world to God. Authority in the life of the church is contingent upon ecclesial events, determined according to the guidelines of contextual methods, the formation of *koinonia*

25. Torrance, *Reality and Evangelical Theology*, 50. Thomas F. Torrance, the son of a Scottish Presbyterian missionary, spent his early years in China. Cf. McGrath, *T. F. Torrance*, 6–10 and 205–11. In his *Karl Barth: Biblical and Evangelical Theologian*, 130, Torrance writes, "All unwarranted presuppositions and every preconceived framework" must be challenged and evaluated in the light of our actual knowledge of God. Quoted by McGrath, ibid., 236. In this way, he argues, the Christian tradition continues to have vitality and intellectual integrity in each context.

and the work of the Holy Spirit. It is not a result of the work of correct belief *per se*. We do not speak with authority without authentic witness, and responsible proclamation and praxis that allows the biblical story to be translated into our lives. The authority of scripture and tradition is worked out in faith and trembling, as we allow Christ to work in our lives through the guidance of the Holy Spirit.

To insist upon a conflict between the Christian scriptures and tradition is to misconstrue the event of revelation and misunderstand the role of the Holy Spirit. Authority is to be located in the activity of the triune God within the community and discipleship of the faithful. Authority within the church is God's work not our work. The mission of the church is God's mission not ours. Authority is given voice through the polyphonic dance of embedded and deliberative theology as the Holy Spirit moves between the Christian scriptures, the church's praxis and beliefs, and the contextual web of the world we occupy. The polyphonic voices of Christian authority are themselves the continuation of the work of Christ in the world.

6

Theology, Both Local and Ecumenical

Tradition and Authority within the Christian Community

THE PARTICULARITY OF CHRISTIAN TRUTH

HISTORICAL AND SOCIAL REALITIES provide textual meaning with its temporal and cultural limits and possibilities. We experience our world because we are part of a world. For our faith to have meaning it must be meaningful in a particular historical, cultural, and social context. The question of whether and how the meaning of the beliefs and practices of Christian faith can be translated into those that share the same truth in other cultures becomes acute. For the claims of Christian conviction to be true they must be commensurable. All this leads to an assertion: once the faith has been shared, it has been communicated across cultures. Different contexts may need to use context-specific language and even different affirmations of faith in order to communicate the same gospel. The definition of theology as faith seeking understanding, however, implies that the gospel can be communicated across cultures. Therefore the faith community is the responsible domain of communication.

Not all scholars are comfortable with these assertions. Roger Haight, for example, put it this way, "Because experience is a function of historical situatedness, the differences of contextual experience show that the meaning of the basic affirmations of Christian faith inevitably changes; the same affirmation in a different context will not mean the same thing and may have little meaning at all."[1] Yet the suggestion that whenever the

1. Haight, *Dynamics of Theology*, 171.

Christian message is shared it becomes a different religion is absurd. We need a subtler understanding of this issue.

To understand this challenge we need to look more closely at the concrete theological process as theological interpretation takes place in community. Local theologians clearly are the ones, who are responsible for interpreting Christian convictions, language, and practice to people. This is the opportunity that contextual theology opens for Christian theology that has gone unrecognized. While scholars in the current context are faced globally with the opportunity of creating global networks which empower the communication of the gospel, it is the local pastor who communicates the gospel. There have long been theologians whose work is primarily research, and pastors whose role is to teach Christian beliefs and practices, proclaim the gospel, and care for communities of faith. What has long been weak is the conversation between the two communities. This has damaged the vitality of churches. The penetration of a helpful theology of mission and evangelism into the language of faith used in local churches has been poor. A new effort should be undertaken.

The classical pattern for discussing the language of faith was that of the ordering of correct teaching or the "deposit of faith." Our beliefs and practices were to align with the rule of faith in order to measure their orthodoxy. The result in our present context has been a hardening of once comprehensible faith into "unquestioned truths." Correct belief becomes a work that is disconnected to what God is doing today. The definition of faith seeking understanding identifies theology as a participation in the *missio Dei*. Therefore, the renewal of our theology makes comprehensible and necessary both a global and a local theological conversation involving scholars, pastors, and local communities.

Paul Lehmann suggested a way to overcome this problem in his proposal for contextual theology. He wrote,

> It belongs to the dialogical character of theology to express and to explicate the Christian referent to which it is committed, in an openness to and confrontation with other perspectives and referents. There is a confessional theology, which is non-dialogical. Such confessionalism seeks to perpetuate the language of theology without sufficient regard to its original context and thus also with insufficient regard to subsequent contexts in which theology must be done. Consequently the dynamic and dialectical interrelation between the referent and the phenomenology

of the Christian community is ignored and the humanizing task of theology is violated. A dialogical confessionalism, however, recognizes that the ultimate test of its humanizing responsibility may well be its hospitality to what it can learn about the genuinely human from other perspectives which do not claim to be what they are not (that is, which do not claim to be theological). The hidden premise of such a dialogical confessionalism is the activity and power of the Holy Spirit.[2]

For example, the doctrines of incarnation and reconciliation circumscribe for the theologian possible theological language use. Concretizing doctrine is part of the pastor's responsibility. Christ's works should be connected to faithful works. Because of Christ's incarnation we are obliged to continue the work that the incarnation began. Jesus' incarnation is the basis for assertions that events in the practices of faith communities make Christ present to people. Because of Jesus Christ's resurrection, we are obliged to see this work in an ecclesial and eschatological perspective. Jesus Christ's ministry shows us the way to do this in that his life was an incarnation of God's will and presence in the world. Christ accepted his culture and sought to transform it. We need to find ways to follow him and continue his work. The cultural is the domain of transformation.

The doctrines of incarnation and reconciliation imply both the universality of the gospel and its particularity. As we have seen, the concretization of the gospel implies that accommodation, translation, and inculturation happen across cultural boundaries. It is Christ's contextualization of the message and reality of salvation through incarnation and reconciliation that communicates the truth about God. This is the work of Christ for the salvation of the world.

We say that the kingdom of God is manifest in the local church when a concrete faith community is a place of *koinonia*. By *koinonia* we understand all that shapes Christian community. Community implies spiritual kinship, unity, sharing, concern for one another, love, forgiveness, and openness to others. In this way, for example, those who suffer have the opportunity of being part of a caring, affirming, loving society of people. This experience is itself therapeutic, healing, and redemptive, as a moment of *kairos*. Clearly this is a concretization of *koinonia*. According to biblical insight, the ministries of a Christian church enact

2. Lehmann, "Doing Theology," 135.

koinonia, diakonia, kerygma, martyria, and *leitourgia.* They are cultural and socially embedded in the beliefs and practices of a people of God. At the same time there are also events that are not ministry, which suppress the means of praxis and inhibit the shaping of helpful and truthful beliefs and practices.

Points of contact and confluence between Christianity and culture need to be uncovered in order to do theology and be Christian.[3] The doctrine of the incarnation argues that God manifests the glory of God and sanctifies the life of this world. Therefore our beliefs and practices, when done for the glory of God, participate in God's mission. In this sense, contextualizing theology disavows the separation of the sacred and profane. There is no place in the world where God is absent.

Yet our knowledge and experience of God transcend context. The fact that we are never condemned to one context, but move from one to another demonstrates this to be true. Something is lost in the process; but something is gained as well. Sometimes such a movement is a struggle. For example, we move from one context to another as we experience change. Change is fundamental to human life. We move through stages of life as a child, as an adolescent, as an adult, and as an elderly person. Our time in life also shapes our experience and knowledge of God. Similarly, the way we understand and live our faith differs as we experience economic, social, political, and cultural change around us. Our common humanity creates for us an opportunity to relate and empathize with people who are distant and different. This sense of our humanity is our kinship. As we struggle against evil so that human life may prevail against the powers of death, we become kin of our global partners in faith. Reconciled communities lead to reconciled lives.

---

3. This can even take the form of non-Christian religious culture, to the extent that the point of contact does not led to the rejection of Christian wisdom. We noted this earlier in our discussion of the Catholic response in the Philippines. We find this repeated in other Asian contexts as well. The position is emphasized among Chinese scholars, who face unique concerns given the history of Protestantism and the impact of modern and Maoist ideologies. The work of Chinese theologian Bishop Shen Yifan has been particularly helpful on this issue. Cf. Yifan, "Confucian Thought and Theological Reflection in China Today," 136–46; Wenfeng, "The Contextualized Theology of Bishop Shen Yifan," 116–22. Bishop Shen Yifan, recently deceased, was committed to the project of contextualizing theology.

LOCAL THEOLOGY AS A LOCUS OF CONTEXTUALIZATION

Because theology is faith seeking understanding, the life of a congregation leads to praxis and cultural mediation. Every congregation develops a communicative praxis as they attempt to live their faith where they are. It is how they become and remain Christians. Theology emerges from action within the community and is not the product of the individual scholar or school of theological thought. It results from partnership elicited by Christian kinship. Paul Lehmann reminds us that commitment to take seriously both the text of belief and the context of Christian living becomes the means to confirm faith. He writes, "Theological positivism is committed to that which *in concreto* elicits its response; that is, it is confessional."[4]

The Spirit of God, who is active in a context, empowers us to see beyond our world. It is the presence of the Spirit that leads us to affirm our faith, as we are called to the spiritual life and confess the beliefs and practices that unite us in Christ. The Spirit's presence is so varied in our shared life that its work is difficult to discern. As Galatians 5 insists, the presence of the God is manifest in the gifts the fruits of Spirit-filled people. In order to discern the presence of the Spirit we have to engage in the praxis of a faith community. Theology is consequently inseparable from the locus of the praxis of a community of believers.

Bernard Lonergan proposes that we study the work of the Holy Spirit in human communities by reflecting on the plethora of meanings and understandings present in a time in order to grasp "what was going forward in particular groups and at particular places and times." In this way, we may discern the work of God who is active "through particular human agents"[5] This vision of the presence of God's Spirit inspiring, leading, calling, and empowering people in all times and places is vital for our understanding of the theological place for contextual methods. An understanding of how God intervenes in history and among peoples is essential. Because the biblical narrative shows God directing people on their journey to the Promised Land, the metaphor of the community of faith as a people of God is essential to an adequate understanding of the nature of the church. One cannot talk about the church without talking about God's presence.

---

4. Lehmann, "Doing Theology," 135.

5. Lonergan, *Doctrinal Pluralism*, 178.

A task of contextual theology is to enable an understanding emerging from a common experience of faith shared by a community of faith in order to share the story of the presence of God in the history of people. Theology discerns the work of God, which is calling peoples on to a journey towards the kingdom of God. Thereby, the community is empowered to praxis by the work of the Holy Spirit.

From this we can see that contextual theology must acknowledge that its truth is universal, for its understanding can only be rendered intelligible and its journey in faith rendered coherent when the context and the text are understood in terms of the Holy Spirit who calls all to have faith and live the Christian life. In this way the intelligible and the coherent elements of the theological process converge as faith becomes understood and engages in praxis. God is calling us all to profess faith in Christ as the one people of God to which all contexts and groups belong.[6]

Consequently, it is necessary to promote understandings of the nature of the church that will encourage a healthy theological process. Accordingly, the church is a community of faith engaged in faithful living and confession. It is the communal articulation and praxis of this faith that manifests the church. Thus the church exists as the community of faith. Both the Roman Catholic and Protestant ecumenical traditions affirm this position today.[7]

There are many barriers to such an understanding of the church. The challenges to *koinonia* come from many aspects of our lives. As I have experienced it in Asia, for example, the plurality of religious groups and communities are alienated from each other as a result of historical ethnic and religious divisions, which have colluded in an ideological hardness of heart. Throughout the world too the church has been a sign of a similar separation through denominationalism and sectarianism. Yet, due to the impact of ecumenical movements, we see fresh trends towards a coming together in Christian purpose and the need for *koinonia*. This is a manifestation of being church, which cannot take place without the empowerment of the theological process that takes the lives of faithful peoples seriously. Perhaps we may discern the prompting of the Spirit urging us to a unity that respects diversity. Perhaps we can see

6. Cf. Eph 4:4–5.

7. Cf. Second Ecumenical Council, *Lumen Gentium*, 8 and World Council of Churches, "The Unity of the Church as *Koinonia*," 124–25.

it rising as peoples struggle to be Christian while becoming more deeply and globally interconnected.[8]

At all times and places the kingdom of God is manifest in the church through the work of the Holy Spirit as congregations seek to live their faith responsibly where they are. In other words, the kingdom becomes manifest as pastoral interpretation leads to concrete ecclesial events. These events of ecclesial praxis express the reality of God's presence within the ministries and institutions of the church. They become means by which we can express and judge praxis. The action of the church in its praxis occurs as culturally mediated pastoral responses. Its reality comes to life as the faithful community seeks to respond to culturally mediated needs and expectations emerging from the context. Events within the church, for example, can be understood as *koinonia* or *kerygma* when they create communal fellowship or initiate responsible proclamation, both events necessary for the identity and life of the church. The goal to live in *koinonia* and proclaim the gospel is manifested as expectations articulated as tradition-bearing theological maxims guiding Christian living. Ministry occurs when pastoral interpretation is mediated.

However, in reflecting on its ministries, the church is always thrown back onto its identity. The ministries are themselves a challenge to the church's self-understanding and the church's identity is a challenge to the cultural and social modes of its ministerial praxis. It is the dialogue of this mutual challenge that informs the church's praxis, which includes an inculturation process, if it is to encourage theological integrity. In this way confessional and local traditions are engaged in the formation of Christian communities.

Given the nature of ecclesial praxis and the vital role of pastoral interpretation, it is important to recognize the process of canonization as essential for Christian community. Without canonical texts, that is, Christian scripture, the faith communities cannot exist. Evangelism and mission depend upon canonization. A community can live the Christian life only if it has embraced Christian scriptures as canon, as the cultur-

---

8. Cf. Segundo, *An Evolutionary Approach to Jesus of Nazareth*, 12. Early in his career Segundo addressed this transformation. He wrote, "we have entered a universal context . . . everything has become interrelated. Our present planetary context of culture will not be replaced by another, nor are there parallel alternatives to it." Segundo is not just referring to the process called globalization. He is recognizing as well the growth of the sense of kinship among peoples around the world. This is especially relevant given the extent of ethnic violence and racism that has so plagued our times.

ally embedded measure for evaluating their beliefs and practices and the source for enriching and defining their traditions.

Pastoral interpretation of biblical sources and texts constitutes the framework for Christian belief. Consequently, the approach we take to biblical interpretation is determinative. This is why we become so uncomfortable with approaches that are different from those we understand and accept. When in the "new Christianity" we discover ways of reading the scriptures that are not reliant on liberal biblical criticism, we are unnerved. Although the project of "reading through the Bible" seems to be over, due to postmodern critique, a literal or "naïve" reading of the scriptures worries us.[9] A similar feeling is shared by both liberal mainstream Western Christianity and fundamentalism. Both liberalism and conservatism had relied upon an appeal to objectivity that could found a universally acceptable and rational system of theology. This is no longer possible, exactly because the house of modernity has collapsed.[10] Yet, many are not glad to see it go and are thrown off balance by the new approaches to biblical interpretation found in the "new Christianity" of the global South. Along with the nervousness has arisen a new awareness of the potential of the theological process to enrich faith communities. The end of rational theological systems has made it possible to construct theologies that are helpful to local Christian communities around the globe.

The process by which the biblical narrative gives form to the theological life of the Christian community is recognized today as the locus for responsible theological work. The task of the theologian is to assist the congregation in a healthy process of reading and responding to the biblical story as canonical scripture. The goal is to retrieve the biblical voice and in the process retrieve healthy local traditions.[11]

9. For a thorough treatment of this issue see Tilley, *History, Theology and Faith*. One of his arguments is that historical work cannot authorize principles of tradition. See especially ibid., 106–27.

10. Allen, *Christian Belief in a Postmodern World*, 1–19.

11. The stained-glassed windows of the Cosmopolitan Church (UCCP) of Malate, Philippines, illustrate the use of biblical and theological tradition in the pastoral care of the congregation. They symbolize the work of the church and are explained to new members as a part of their inclusion in their congregation. They symbolize *martyria, koinonia, diakonia, kerygma, and leitourgia*. The following wisdom is passed on. It is explained in the following way. In *martyria*, the Church witnesses to its faith in the risen Lord and people give their lives to and for the Lord to allow his kingdom to be manifest through them. In *koinonia* the people of God manifest the essential communal

This effort to retrieve the biblical voice is meant to recover a tradition identified often with the Reformation and the principle of *sola scriptura*. According to this tradition, the point of departure is scripture as the norming norm. The Westminster Confession is one of the most definitive statements of this point of departure. Scripture is the "Supreme Judge, by which all controversies of religion are to be determined."[12] It is "the Holy Spirit that speaks in the Scripture." Authority lies in the Holy Spirit speaking in and through the scripture. Because the Holy Spirit speaks through scripture, it has authority. For many these statements are irrevocable and constitute traditions essential for Christian living.

The locus for theological reflection is the enlivening of our hearing of the biblical story through the Holy Spirit. The *locus classicus* for this is 2 Timothy 3:16–17. God breathes into the scripture. The author of 2 Timothy uses the concept of *theopneustos* to make his point. Augustine recovered this when he spoke of the living word and the dead letter. The Reformers thought of their work as the recovery of the real Christian tradition. To hear God's Word through the Christian scriptures is to listen to the Spirit's voice.

At the heart of this conviction is the belief that the Spirit guides the Christian community. It is based upon the anticipation of God's continued involvement in the life of Christian communities. Consequently, the Bible is canonical scripture in that we are a listening and confessing people. The Bible has authority when the story, the message about God, is heard and the work of Christ continues among the community of faithful believers. The original intent of the principles of *sola scriptura* and *norma normata* is to focus on this event as the locus for theological reflection. Only with this focus recovered can the Bible be the formative source for theological construction and a guide for authentic witness and responsible proclamation.

In the context of a global Christianity it is no longer possible to identify the principles of *sola scriptura* and *norma normata* as Protestant. They have become traditions of every faith community—Protestant,

---

nature of God's kingdom, living the truth of being one body in one Lord. In *diakonia* the kingdom is realized through the command to love and serve others and in particular the poor. In *kerygma* the kingdom is proclaimed as good news for the people of all places, times, and contexts. In *leitourgia* the kingdom is celebrated as the living presence of God amongst his people through worship and prayer. Their Christian faith is passed on in that it is embedded in the art and architecture of their place of worship.

12. *The Westminster Confession of Faith*, 1.10.

Orthodox, evangelical, and Roman Catholic—around the world where the biblical story is told and the gospel is heard.

TELLING AND HEARING THE BIBLICAL STORY AS EVENTS OF THEOLOGICAL PRAXIS

The contexts of the biblical texts are remote both historically and personally. We do not read it as our story until we acknowledge it as a story that occurred in a different historical and cultural context from our own. This recognition has given rise to a new emphasis in interpretation on contextual reality. The community develops a strategy for listening that acknowledges the text's own integrity. The otherness or strangeness of the text, as Karl Barth described it, reminds us of the distance between our world and the world of the text. We should not alter the text so that fits into our world. The text as a part of the biblical story has its own integrity. There is an inevitable clash between our culturally embedded perspective and that of the text. Theological hermeneutics does not attempt to fuse the two worlds, but rather to open up a new perspective on the reader's world—its culture and context. It invites and calls the reader to inhabit their world as seen from an eschatological perspective. This is what is meant by spiritual engagement with a text. Reading and listening to a text within the community of faith invites the Spirit to work among the faithful.

The conviction that is reinforced by the principle of *sola scriptura* is that a Spirit-engaged reading of the text will hinder the misuse of the text. By reading the Bible theologically, the unity of the purposefulness of God takes shape. It becomes canon. This unity or canonicity constitutes an interpretive center for interpreting both the Old and New Testaments as biblical witness, as scripture, and as the source for biblical and Christian wisdom. While the distinctive voices of the Bible express a polyphony of theological perspectives, the Bible is more than any individual voice. It is more than just a list of the mighty acts of God, as Gerhard von Rad was wont to say.[13] Each voice serves as a promise of insight into eschatological reality. To evaluate this point, David Dawson speaks of a triadic perspective. When we read the text in community, we are part of a hermeneutical event that places the readers of the text in

---

13. Cf. Von Rad, *Old Testament Theology*.

relation to God and to each other.[14] The hope that is shared with Israel through the Exodus is the same hope that we experience in our own baptism and within our ministry as faithful believers. This is not just a metaphor for a relation between the past and present. It is a metonymic relation, in that both ancient Israel and contemporary Christians stand in relation to the same God—the God they believe in. The understanding of this event by ancient Israel is not irrelevant or redundant. It is highly meaningful because we conceive of God from an eschatological perspective informed by the biblical story as a whole.

FAITH COMMUNITIES ARE PLACES
FOR THEOLOGICAL REFLECTION

Recalling an earlier point, we can return to the role of the Spirit's voice in theological work. According to our argument, the Holy Spirit forms Christian community through the proclamation of the biblical witness. A faithful community seeks to live the biblical narrative in its historical, cultural, and social context. The goal of our listening to the literature of the Bible is to hear the Spirit's voice forming us according to God's purposes. When we listen, we are participating in God's mission for the world.

Hearing the Spirit's voice, the community acknowledges the Christian traditions that have been formed through the history of Christianity. We come to hear the text as participants in this traditioning process. Awareness of our place within this process is helpful in that it makes us aware of the interpretative traditions that we have inherited and are part of our history as a faith community. We read and listen like others before us who have sought to be Christ's disciples. The local church develops wise leaders who help us hear the Spirit's voice.

We must also hear the biblical story as inhabitants of social and cultural contexts and participants in specific faith communities. In doing so we are asking the Spirit to help us understand what God is expecting of us in our place among the peoples of the globe. It is the case that any effort to engage in the theological task is both local and global. The polyphony of the many voices of the faith communities of the world as they seek to discern the workings of the Spirit among them is in reality a

14. Dawson, *Literary Theory*, 29. Dale Martin in his recent book entitled *Pedagogy of the Bible* gives some indication of what this and similar approaches to biblical interpretation might mean for contemporary theological formation in the West.

source for our own discernment. Just as they are asking for guidance in their location, we too are asking the same God the same question. How can we be disciples where we are, being who we are? In that God is working throughout the world, by hearing what the Spirit is saying globally we can learn about the call to serve, proclaim, and witness locally.

Being responsible Christians means above all being responsible members of a faith community—a local church with a global reach. We can only come to the Christian scriptures as participants in a visible fellowship of disciples in covenant with the one God in Jesus Christ. Through the activity of the Holy Spirit, God is envisioning our future as participants in the work of divine mission for the world. We cannot do this without engaging in the hermeneutical task of theological praxis. It is central to the traditioning process of all responsible faith communities that they are seeking the Spirit's voice. At the heart of a faithful community's life is the active engagement in responsible proclamation and witness. The praxis and theology of the Christian community depends upon this engagement for its life and for its convictions concerning reality.

Without contextual methods, neither faithful praxis nor theological reflection can happen. We cannot become a fellowship in abstraction. We become a fellowship because God has a vision for us, for every congregation and believer, which through the activity of the Holy Spirit, becomes a reality manifested in ecclesial events. Contextual methods make it possible for these events to become the church confessing faith in Jesus Christ.

THE ECUMENICAL AND CONTEXTUAL CHURCH IN THE FULLNESS OF FAITH

When Shoki Coe and others recommended the use of contextual methods several decades ago, they did not do so with the hope of creating greater division among an already tragically divided Christianity. They did so with the conviction that contextual theology would create contextual churches, united in their faith in Christ and freed from the ties of ethnicity, denominationalism, and racism. They hoped that contextual methods would break down the hothouse of effect whereby churches in the global South were simply transplanted institutions from the West. By overcoming the divide that had alienated concrete context and biblical text, the hope was that faith in Christ would no longer be perceived as the faith of foreigners, but had found a home everywhere.

The problem of contextualization is always related to the ecumenical debate exactly because it impacts our understanding of the nature of the church. The use of contextual methods leads ultimately to contextual churches, with different theologies, visions, and biblical interpretations. Lack of attention to context can lead to disunity and the continuation of painful ethnic and denominational divisions. It can lead to hatred and violence between Christians and neighbors.

Christian communities are called to Shalom. Contextual theology is intent upon renewal of faith communities according to God's purposes so that Shalom can reign. This is certainly the best test of the authenticity of a Christian community. Contextualization, when properly conceived and applied, is the means to ensure authenticity. It does more than just share the Good News; it participates in the work of the Holy Spirit planting healthy Christian communities among all peoples. Christian unity cannot be transplanted. It grows wherever it takes root through faith seeking understanding. The unity of the church is visible in the lives of faithful communities. The true drama of our times is not the ethnic and racist violence that dominates our news, but the renewal of Christian communities that is taking place across the globe.

Bibliography

Ainslie III, Peter. *Toward Christian Unity*. Baltimore: Association for the Promotion of Christian Unity, 1918.

Allen, Diogenes. *Christian Belief in a Postmodern World: The Full Wealth of Conviction*. Louisville: Westminster John Knox, 1989.

Anderson, Gerald. "American Protestants in Pursuit of Mission." In *Missiology: An Ecumenical Introduction*, edited by Frans J. Verstraelen, et al., 374–420. Grand Rapids: Eerdmans, 1995.

———, editor. *Asian Voices in Christian Theology*. Maryknoll, NY: Orbis, 1976.

———. "Providence and Politics behind Protestant Missionary Beginnings in the Philippines." In *Studies in Philippine Church History*, edited by Gerald H. Anderson, 279–300. Ithaca, NY: Cornell University Press, 1969.

Appiah-Kubi, Kofi, and Sergio Torres, editors. *African Theology en Route*. Maryknoll, NY: Orbis, 1979.

Assmann, Jan. *Religion and Cultural Memory*. Stanford: Stanford University Press, 2006.

Barrows, John Henry. *The Christian Conquest of Asia: Studies and Personal Observations of Oriental Religions*. New York: Scribners, 1899.

Barth, Karl. "Barth's Last Pastoral Letter." *The South East Asia Journal of Theology* 2 (Autumn 1969) 117–36.

———. *Evangelical Theology: An Introduction*. New York: Holt, Rineheart, Winston, 1963.

Bellah, Robert. "Religious Evolution." *American Sociological Review* 29 (1964) 358–74.

Berger, Peter. "Four Faces of Global Culture." In *Globalization and the Challenges of the New Century: A Reader*, edited by Patrick O'Meara, et al., 419–27. Indianapolis: Indiana University Press, 2000.

———. "The Cultural Dynamics of Globalization." In *Many Globalizations: Cultural Diversity in the Contemporary World*, edited by Peter Berger and Samuel Huntington, 16. New York: Oxford University Press, 2002.

Bevans, Stephen B. "A Local Theology in a World Church." *New Theology Review* 1 (Feb 1988).

———. *An Introduction to Theology in Global Perspective*. Maryknoll, NY: Orbis, 2009.

———. *Models of Contextual Theology*. Revised and expanded. Maryknoll, NY: Orbis, 2002.

Bevans, Stephen B., and Roger P. Schroeder. *Constants in Context: A Theology of Mission for Today*. Maryknoll, NY: Orbis, 2004.

Boff, Clovodis. "Epistemology and Method of the Theology of Liberation." In *Mysterium Liberationis: Fundamental Concepts of Liberation Theology*, edited by Ignacio Ellacuría and Jon Sobrino, 62–80. Maryknoll, NY: Orbis, 1993.

———. *Theology and Praxis: Epistemological Foundations*. Translated by Robert Barr. Maryknoll, NY: Orbis, 1987.

Boff, Leonardo. *When Theology Listens to the Poor.* Translated by Robert R. Barr. San Francisco: Harper & Row, 1988.

Bonhoeffer, Dietrich. "Memorandum: The Social Gospel." In *Berlin 1932–1933: Dietrich Bonhoeffer Works,* edited by Larry Rasmussen, 236–42. Dietrich Bonhoeffer Works, vol. 12. Minneapolis, MN: Fortress, 2009.

———. *Widerstand und Ergebung.* Edited by Christian Gremmels, et al. Dietrich Bonhoeffer Werke 8. Gütersloh: Kaiser, 1998.

Bosch, David J. *Transforming Mission: Paradigm Shifts in Theology of Mission.* Maryknoll, NY: Orbis, 1991.

Braaten, Carl. *Flaming Center: A Theology of the Christian Mission.* Philadelphia: Fortress, 1977.

———. *Mother Church: Ecclesiology and Ecumenism.* Minneapolis: Fortress, 1998.

———. *That All May Believe: A Theology of the Gospel and the Mission of the Church.* Grand Rapids: Eerdmans, 2008.

Braaten, Carl E., and Robert W. Jenson. *Strange New Word of the Gospel: Re-evangelizing in the Postmodern World.* Grand Rapids: Eerdmans, 2002.

Brown, Robert McAfee. "The Rootedness of All Theology: Context Affects Content." *Christianity and Crisis* 37 (July 18, 1977) 170–74.

Burtness, James. "Innovation as a Search for Probabilities: To Re-contextualize the Text." In *Learning in Context.* Bromily Kent: Theological Education Fund, 1973.

Chomsky, Noam, and Michel Foucault. *The Chomsky-Foucault Debate on Human Nature.* New York: The New Press, 2006.

Coe, Shoki. "Contextualization as the Way Toward Reform." In *Asian Christian Theology— Emerging Themes,* edited by Douglas J. Elwood, 48–55. Philadelphia: Westminster, 1980.

———. "Contextualizing Theology." In *Mission Trends, No.3: Third World Theologies,* edited by G. H. Anderson and T. F. Stransky, 19–24. Grand Rapids: Eerdmans, 1976.

———. "In Search of Renewal in Theological Education." *Theological Education* 9 (Summer 1973) 233–43.

Comaroff, John, and Jean Comaroff. *Ethnicity, Inc.* Chicago: University of Chicago Press, 2009.

Cone, James. "The Social Context of Theology." In *Doing Theology Today,* edited by C. S. Song, 17–41. Madras: The Christian Literature Society, 1976.

Costa, Ruy O., editor. *One Faith, Many Cultures: Inculturation, Indigenization, and Contextualization.* Maryknoll, NY: Orbis, 1988.

Cruz, Oscar. "Pastoral Exhortation on Philippine Culture." In *CBCP: On the Threshold of the Next Millennium,* 194ff. Manila: Catholic Bishops' Conference of the Philippines, 1999.

Dawson, David. *Literary Theory.* Guides to Theological Inquiry. Minneapolis: Fortress, 1995.

De Gruchy, John W. *Theology and Ministry in Context and Crisis.* London: Collins, 1986.

De Mesa, José. "Being Mindful of Context: Characterizing "Contextual Theology." In *Charting the Future of Theology and Theological Education in Asian Contexts,* edited by David Kwang-sun Suh, et al, 244ff. Delhi: ISPCK, 2004.

———. *In Solidarity with Culture: Studies in Theological Re-rooting.* Quezon City, Philippines: Maryhill School of Theology, 1987.

———. *Why Theology is Never Far From Home.* Manila: De La Salle University Press, 2003.

De Mesa, José, and Lode Wostyn, *Doing Theology: Basic Realities and Processes*. Quezon City, Philippines: Claretian, 1990.

Duby, Georges. *The Three Orders: Feudal Society Imagined*. Chicago: University of Chicago Press, 1980.

Dulles, Avery. *Models of Revelation*. Maryknoll, NY: Orbis, 1992.

Dussel, Enrique. *The Underside of Modernity: Apel, Ricoeur, Rorty, Taylor and the Philosophy of Liberation*. New Jersey: Humanities, 1996.

Elwood, Douglas, editor. *Asian Christian Theology*. Philadelphia: Fortress, 1980.

FABC Documents. Federation of Asian Bishops Conference, Calcutta, 1978.

Ferguson, Niall. *War of the World: History's Age of Hatred*. London: Lane, 2006.

Fernandez, Eleazar. *Reimagining the Human: Theological Anthropology in Response to Systemic Evil*. St. Louis: Chalice, 2004.

Foucault, Michel. *Naissance de la biopolitique: Cours au College de France, 1978–79*. Edition tablie sous la direction de François Ewald et Alessandro, par Michel Senellart. Paris: Gallimard, Seuil, 2004.

Fuellenbach, John. *The Kingdom of God*. Manila: Divine Word, 1987.

Gay, Peter. *The Enlightenment: An Interpretation. The Rise of Modern Paganism*. New York: Knopf, 1966.

Geertz, Clifford. *Interpretation of Cultures: Selected Essays*. New York: Basic, 1973.

———. *Local Knowledge: Further Essays in Interpretive Anthropology*. New York: Basic, 1983.

Gichure, Peter Ignatius. *Contextual Theology: Its Meaning, Scope and Urgency*. Nairobi: The Catholic University of Eastern Africa, 2008.

Gutiérrez, Gustavo. *Las Casas: In Search of the Poor of Jesus Christ*. Translated by Robert Barr. Maryknoll, NY: Orbis, 1993.

———. *The God of Life*. Translated by Matthew J. O'Connell. Maryknoll, NY: Orbis, 1991.

———. "God's Revelation and Proclamation in History." In *The Power of the Poor in History*. Translated by Robert Barr. Maryknoll, NY: Orbis, 1983.

Habermas, Jürgen. *The Structural Transformation of the Public Sphere*. Translated by Thomas Burger. Studies in Contemporary German Social Thought. Cambridge, MA: MIT Press, 1989.

———. *Theory of Communicative Action*. Two Volumes. Translated by Thomas McCarthy. Boston: Beacon, 1987.

Haight, Roger. *An Alternative Vision: An Interpretation of Liberation Theology*. New York: Paulist, 1985.

———. *Dynamics of Theology*. New York: Paulist, 1990.

Hall, Douglas John. *Thinking the Faith: Christian Theology in a North American Context*. Minneapolis, MN: Augsburg/Fortress, 1989.

Hanciles, Jehu J. *Beyond Christendom: Globalization, African Migration, and the Transformation of the West*. Maryknoll, NY: Orbis, 2008.

Hesselgrave, David J. and Edward Rommen. *Contextualization: Meanings, Methods, and Models*. Grand Rapids: Baker, 1989.

Hiebert, Paul G. *Gospel in Human Contexts: Anthropological Explorations for Contemporary Mission*. Grand Rapids: Baker Academic, 2009.

———. *Transforming Worldviews: An Anthropological Understanding of How People Change*. Grand Rapids: Baker Academic, 2008.

Hunsberger, George. *Bearing the Witness of the Spirit: Lesslie Newbigin's Theology of Cultural Plurality.* Grand Rapids: Eerdmans, 1998.

Irvin, Dale. *Christian Histories, Christian Traditioning: Rendering Accounts.* Maryknoll, NY: Orbis, 1998.

Jenkins, Philip. *The New Faces of Christianity: Believing the Bible in the Global South.* New York: Oxford University Press, 2006.

———. *The Next Christendom: The Coming of Global Christianity.* New York: Oxford University Press, 1999.

John Paul II. Encyclical Letter, On Commitment to Ecumenism *Ut Unum Sint* (May 25, 1995). Pasay City, Philippines: Paulines Publishing, 1996.

———. Encyclical Letter, On the Permanent Validity of the Church's Missionary Mandate *Redemptoris Missio* (December 7, 1990). Pasay City, Philippines: Paulines Publishing, 1991.

Jones, Serene, and Paul Lakeland, editors. *Constructive Theology: A Contemporary Approach to Classical Themes.* Minneapolis: Fortress, 2005.

Jose, Joselito Alviar. "The Future of Filipino Theology." In *The Rise of Filipino Theology*, edited by Dindo Rei M. Tesoro and Joselito Alviar Jose, 256–69. Paasay City, Philippines: Paulines, 2004.

Kähler, Martin. *Schriften zur Christologie und Mission. Gesamtausgabe der Schriften zur Mission*, edited by Heinzgünter Frohnes. Munich: Kaiser, 1971.

Käsemann, Ernest. "The Beginnings of Christian Theology." In *New Testament Questions of Today.* Translated by W. I. Montague. Philadelphia: Fortress, 1969.

Kalilombe, Patrick-Augustine. *Doing Theology at the Grassroots: Theological Essays from Malawi.* Gweru, Zimbabwe: Mambo, 1999.

———. "Third World Theologies: A Challenge to Peace Programmes." Oxford Project for Peace Studies, Paper 4. Oxford, OPPS, 1988.

Kelsey, David. *Eccentric Existence: A Theological Anthropology.* Vol. 1. Louisville: Westminster John Knox, 2009.

Kierkegaard, Søren. *Attack Upon Christendom.* Translated by Walter Lowrie. Boston: Beacon, 1956.

Kinsler, F. Ross. "Mission and Context." *Evangelical Missions Quarterly* 14 (Jan 1974) 23–29.

Kipling, Rudyard. "To Take Up the White Man's Burden." *McClure's Magazine* 12 (Feb 1899) 290.

Koyama, Kosuke. "Reflections on Associations of Theological Schools in Southeast Asia." *Southeast Asia Journal of Theology* 15 (1974) 10–25.

Kraft, Charles. *Christianity and Culture: A Study in Dynamic Biblical Theologizing in Cross-Cultural Perspective.* Maryknoll, NY: Orbis, 1981.

Kuhn, Thomas S. *The Structure of Scientific Revolutions.* Chicago: University of Chicago, 1970.

Lam, Wing-Hung. *Chinese Theology in Construction.* Pasadena, CA: William Carey Library, 1983.

Larom, Margaret S., editor. *Claiming the Promise: African Churches Speak.* New York: Friendship, 1994.

Lehmann, Paul Louis. "On Doing Theology: A Contextual Possibility." In *Prospect for Theology. Essays in Honour of H. H. Farmer*, edited by F. G. Healey, 119–36. Digswell Place, Hertfordshire: Nisbet, 1966.

———. "Willingen and Lund: The Church on the Way to Unity." *Theology Today* 9 (1953) 431–41.

Link, Hans-Georg. *Apostolic Faith Today: Handbook for Study*. Geneva: World Council of Churches, 1985.

Lonergan, Bernard. *Doctrinal Pluralism*. Milwaukee: Marquette University Press, 1971.

———. *Method in Theology*. London: Darton, Longman & Todd, 1971.

Maggay, Melba. *The Gospel in Filipino Context*. Manila: OFM, 1987.

Martin, Dale. *Pedagogy of the Bible: An Analysis and Proposal*. Louisville: Westminster John Knox, 2008.

Matheny, Paul. *The Theology of Christian Churches*. Quezon City: Philippines, 2011.

McGrath, Alister E. *T. F. Torrance: An Intellectual Biography*. Edinburgh: T. & T. Clark, 1999.

Metz, Johann-Baptist. *Theology of the World*. New York: Herder & Herder, 1969.

Metz, Johann-Baptist, and Edward Schillebeeckx, editors. *World Catechism or Inculturation?* London: Concilium, 2004.

Mignolo, Walter D. *Local Histories / Global Designs*. Princeton: Princeton University Press, 2000.

Milbank, John. *Theology and Social Theory*. 2nd ed. Oxford: Blackwell, 2006.

Minear, Paul. "Ecumenical Theology—Profession or Vocation?" In *Doing Theology Today*, edited by Choan-Seng Song, 1–16. Madras: Christian Literature Society, 1976.

———. *Images of the Church in the New Testament*. Philadelphia, Westminster, 1960.

Minutes of the Senate of SEAGST, Bangkok, February 1972.

Minutes of the Senate of SEAGST, GS 7209, 1972.

Moltmann, Jürgen. *The Trinity and the Kingdom: The Doctrine of God*. Translated by Margaret Kohl. New York: Harper & Row, 1981.

Mott, John R. *The Evangelization of the World in this Generation*. London: Student Volunteer Movement for Foreign Missions, 1900.

———, editor. *Evangelism for the World Today: As Interpreted by Christian Leaders throughout the World*. New York: Published for the International Missionary Council by Harper & Brothers, 1938.

Nature of the Unity We Seek. Official Report of the North American Conference on Faith and Order, September 3–10, 1957, Oberlin, Ohio. Edited by Paul Minear. St. Louis: Bethany, 1958.

Newbigin, Lesslie. *Foolishness to the Greeks: The Gospel and Western Culture*. London: SPCK, 1986.

———. *The Gospel in a Pluralist Society*. London: SPCK, 1989.

———. "What is 'a Local Church Truly United?' 1976." In *The Ecumenical Movement: An Anthology of Key Texts and Voices*, edited by Michael Kinnamon and Brian Cope, 114–21 Geneva: WCC, 1997.

Nida, Eugene A. *Message and Mission: The Communication of the Christian Faith*. New York: Harper & Row, 1960.

Nida, Eugene, and William D. Reyburn, *Meaning across Cultures*. Maryknoll, NY: Orbis, 1981.

Niles, Preman. "Towards a Framework of Doing Theology in Asia." *Asia Focus* (1977) 16–28.

Noll, Mark A. *The New Shape of World Christianity: How American Experience Reflects Global Faith*. InterVarsity Academic, 2009.

Oracion, Levi. *Human Realizations of Grace*. Cebu City, Philippines: Strongwaters, 2005.

Orevillo-Montenegro, Muriel. *The Jesus of Asian Women: Women from the Margins*. Maryknoll, NY: Orbis, 2006.

Paul VI, Apostolic Exhortation *Evangelii Nuntiandi*, (December 8, 1975) no. 129, in *Vatican Council II: More Post-Conciliar Documents*, edited by Austin P Flannery,

OP, 711-761. New Revised Edition. Pasay City, Philippines: Paulines Publishing House, 1984.

Pinker, Stephen. *The Blank Slate: The Modern Denial of Human Nature.* New York: Viking, 2002.

Placher, William. *Unapologetic Theology.* Louisville: Westminster John Knox, 1989.

Plantinga, Alvin. "The Reformed Objection to Natural Theology." In *Philosophy of Religion,* edited by Michael L. Peterson. Oxford: Oxford University Press, 1996.

―――. *Warranted Christian Belief.* New York: Oxford University Press, 2000.

Ricoeur, Paul. *Hermeneutics and the Human Sciences.* Cambridge: Cambridge University Press, 1981.

―――. *Oneself as Another.* Translated by Kathlenn Blamey. Chicago: University of Chicago Press, 1992.

Ritschl, Dietrich. *The Logic of Theology.* Translated by John Bowden. Minneapolis: Fortress, 1991.

Ro, Bong Rin, and Ruth Eschenauer, editors. *The Bible and Theology in Asian Contexts.* Taichung, Taiwan: Asia Theological Association, 1984.

Roest, A. Crollius. "Inculturation and the Meaning of Culture." *Gregorianum* 61 (1980) 253–74.

Rorty, Richard. *Philosophy and Social Hope.* London: Penguin, 1999.

Russel, Letty, editor. *Changing Contexts of Our Faith.* Philadelphia: Fortress, 1985.

Rütti, Ludwig. *Zur Theologie der Mission: Kritischen Analysen und neue Orientierungen* Munich: Kaiser, 1972.

Sanneh, Lamin. *Disciples of All Nations: Pillars of World Christianity.* Maryknoll, NY: Orbis, 2008.

―――. *Translating the Message.* 2nd ed. Maryknoll, NY: Orbis, 2009.

―――. *Whose Religion is Christianity? The Gospel beyond the West.* Grand Rapids: Eerdmans, 2003.

Sauter, Gerhard. "How Can Theology Derive from Experience?" In *Doing Theology Today,* edited by Choan-Seng Song, 70–89. Madras: Christian Literature Society, 1976.

Schillebeeckx, Edward. *God the Future of Man.* London: Sheed & Ward, 1969.

Schreiter, Robert J. *Constructing Local Theologies.* Maryknoll, NY: Orbis, 1985.

―――. *The New Catholicity: Theology between the Global and the Local.* Maryknoll, NY: Orbis, 1997.

Schineller, Peter. *A Handbook on Inculturation.* New York: Paulist, 1990.

Second Vatican Ecumenical Council. *Ad Gentes Divinitus* (December 7, 1965), no. 61, in *Vatican Council II: The Conciliar and Post-Conciliar Documents,* edited by Austin P. Flannery, OP, 813–56. New Revised Edition. Pasay City, Philippines: Paulines, 1984.

―――. Pastoral Constitution on the Church in the Modern World *Gaudium et Spes* (December 7, 1965), no. 64, in *Vatican Council II: The Conciliar and Post-Conciliar Documents,* edited by Austin P. Flannery, OP, 903–1001. New Revised Edition. Pasay City, Philippines: Paulines, 1984.

―――. Dogmatic Constitution on the Church, *Lumen Gentium* (November 21, 1964) no. 28, in *Vatican Council II: The Conciliar and Post-Conciliar Documents,* edited by Austin P. Flannery, OP, 350–440. New Revised Edition. Pasay City, Philippines: Paulines, 1984.

―――. Decree on Ecumenism *Unitatis redintegratio* (November 21, 1964), no. 32, in *Vatican Council II: The Conciliar and Post-Conciliar Documents,* edited by Austin

P Flannery, OP, 452–70. New Revised Edition. Pasay City, Philippines: Paulines, 1984.

Segundo, Juan Luis. *An Evolutionary Approach to Jesus of Nazareth*. Edited and translated by John Drury. Maryknoll, NY: Orbis, 1988.

Shorter, Aylward. *Toward a Theology of Inculturation*. London: Chapmann, 1988.

Skreslet, Stanley. *Picturing Christian Witness*. Grand Rapids: Eerdmans, 2006.

Sobrino, Jon. *Where is God? Earthquake, Terrorism, Barbarity, and Hope*. Maryknoll, NY: Orbis, 2004.

Soskice, Janet Martin. "The Truth Looks Different from Here or On Seeking the Unity of Truth from a Diversity of Perspectives." In *Christ and Context*, edited by Hilary Regan and Alan J. Torrance, 43–59. Edinburgh: T. & T. Clark, 1993.

Stackhouse, Max. "Contextualization, Contextuality and Contextualism." In *One Faith, Many Cultures*, edited by R. O. Costa, 3–13. Maryknoll, NY: Orbis, 1988.

Suk, John, editor. *Doing Theology in the Philippines. First Annual Asian Theological Seminary Forum on Theology*. Manila: OMF, 2005.

Takenaka, Masao. *God is Rice: Asian Culture and Christian Faith*. Geneva: World Council of Churches, 1986.

Tanner, Kathryn. *Theories of Culture: A New Agenda for Theology*. Guides to Theological Inquiry. Minneapolis: Fortress, 1996.

Tanner, Kathryn, et al, editors. *Converging on Culture: Theologians in Dialogue with Cultural Analysis and Criticism*. New York: Oxford University Press, 2001.

Tano, Rodrigo. *Theology in the Philippine Setting: A Case Study in the Contextualization of Theology*. Quezon City, Philippines: New Day, 1981.

———. *This Complicated and Risky Task: Selected Essays on Doing Contextual Theology from a Filipino Evangelical Perspective*. Edited by Romel R. Bagares. Quezon City, Philippines: Centralbooks, 2006.

Taylor, Charles. *Modern Social Imaginaries*. Durham: Duke University Press, 2004.

———. *A Secular Age*. Cambridge: Belknap, 2007.

Theological Education Fund Staff. *Ministry in Context*. Bromley, UK: Theological Education Fund, 1972.

———. *Learning in Context*. Bromley, UK: Theological Education Fund, 1973.

Temple, William. *The Church Looks Forward*. New York: Macmillan, 1944.

The Third World Conference on Faith and Order Council, Lund 1952, edited by Oliver Tomkins. London: SCM, 1952.

Tilley, Terrence W. *History, Theology and Faith: Dissolving the Modern Problematic*. Maryknoll, NY: Orbis, 2004.

Torrance, Thomas F. *Reality and Evangelical Theology*. Philadelphia: Westminster, 1982.

Van Dusen, Henry P. *World Christianity: Yesterday, Today, Tomorrow*. New York: Abingdon-Cokesbury, 1947.

Vanhoozer, Kevin J., editor. *The Cambridge Companion to Postmodern Theology*. Cambridge: Cambridge University Press, 2003.

Vela, Jesús Andrés. "Un modelo de formación de agentes pastorales en América Latina." *Theologica Xaveriana* 71 (1984) 141–63.

Vischer, Lukas. *Intercession*. Faith and Order Paper, no. 95. Geneva: World Council of Churches Publications, 1980.

Visser 't Hooft, W. A. *The Background of the Social Gospel*. Haarlem: Netherlands, 1928.

———. "Evangelism in the Neo-Pagan Situation." *International Review of Mission* 63 (Jan 1974) 81–86.

Volf, Miroslav, and Dorothy Bass, editors. *Practicing Theology: Beliefs and Practices in Christian Life.* Grand Rapids: Eerdmans, 2002.

Von Allmen, Daniel. "The Birth of Theology: Contextualization as the Dynamic Element in the Formation of New Testament Theology." *International Review of Mission* 64 (Jan 1975) 37–52.

Wainwright, Geoffrey. "The Global Structures of Ecumenism." In *The Ecumenical Future*, edited by Carl Braaten and Robert W. Jenson, 11–28. Grand Rapids: Eerdmans, 2004.

Wallenstein, Immanuel. *The Modern World-System.* 3 vols. London: Academic, 1974, 1980, 1989.

Walls, Andrew. *The Cross-Cultural Process in Christian History.* Maryknoll, NY: Orbis, 2002.

———. *The Missionary Movement in Christian History: Studies in the Transmission of the Faith.* Maryknoll, NY: Orbis, 1996.

Wei, Francis C. M. *The Spirit of Chinese Culture.* New York: Scribner, 1947.

Wenfeng, Ouyang. "The Contextualized Theology of Bishop Shen Yifan." *Nanjing Theological Review* 2 (2003) 116–22.

World Council of Churches. *Confessing the One Faith: Faith and Order Paper No. 153.* Geneva: World Council of Churches, 1991.

———. *Gathered for Life: Official Report, Sixth Assembly, World Council of Churches.* Edited by David Gill. Grand Rapids: Eerdmans, 1983.

———. *Old and New in the Church. Faith and Order Study.* Edited by Paul S. Minear. Minneapolis: Augsburg, 1961.

———. "The Unity of the Church as Koinonia: Gift and Calling." Seventh Assembly of the World Council of Churches, Canberra, 1991. In *The Ecumenical Movement: An Anthology of Key Texts and Voices,* edited by Michael Kinnamon and Brian Cope, 124–25. Grand Rapids: Eerdmans, 1997.

———. *Uppsala Assembly. Drafts for Sections,* Second Section. Geneva: World Council of Churches, 1967.

Yifan, Shen. "Confucian Thought and Theological Reflection in China Today." In *Confucian-Christian Encounters in Historical and Contemporary Perspective,* edited by Peter K. H. Lee, 136–46. New York: Mellen, 1991.

Subject Index

acculturation, 33, 38
Ad Gentes, 21, 27n14, 33n27, 67,
    69n26, 74, 75, 75n32
adaption, 35, 74
analysis, metalinguistic, 37
anthropology
    contemporary, 26, 32
    cultural, 38
    modern, 38
    theological, 48
ascesis, 89, 89n6
Association of Theological
    Education of South East Asia
    (ATESEA), *xiv*
atonement, 9
authority, scriptural, 9, 20, 36, 56,
    103, 112
axioms, fluid, 102

canon, 53, 54, 56, 57, 78, 84, 87, 90,
    90n10, 101, 110, 112
canonization, 53, 90n10, 110, 113
Catechism for Filipino Catholics, 76
Catholic Bishops' Conference of the
    Philippines (CBCP), 75–76
Christendom, 4–9, 13, 15, 16, 37,
    41, 75
Christian Century, 2, 2n3
Christianity, global, *xv*, 1, 4, 91, 112
Christianity, new, *x*, *xi*, *xin1*, *xii*, 4,
    5, 17, 18, 20, 21, 23, 38, 43, 59,
    61, 80, 81, 91, 92, 111
Christianity, world, *xiii*, 2, 75

Christology, *xii*, 9, 10, 28n9, 42, 57,
    67
church
    contextual, 96, 98, 115, 116
    local, *x*, *xv*, 12, 15, 23, 28, 33, 55,
        70, 74, 78, 94, 96, 97, 100, 105,
        106, 114, 115
    medieval, 6
    missionary, 6, 7, 14, 75
civilization, 3, 5, 69n19, 94
codes, cultural, 34, 40n42
commensurability, *xii*, 41, 51, 81
colonialism, *ix*, *xiv*, 1, 2, 5n10, 13,
    47, 47n6, 68
condition, human, 21, 29, 51, 65
contextuality, 21, 30, 70, 70n21, 98
contextualization, *ix*, *xivn6*, 9, 15,
    25, 26, 29, 30, 34, 35, 35n32,
    36, 38, 45, 46, 57, 63n6, 64n8,
    67, 70, 70n21, 72, 74, 78, 79,
    91, 95n16, 97–99, 106, 116
Council of Christian Union
    (COCU), 2, 2n3
Critical Asian Principle, *xiv*, *xivn6*
culture
    local, *ix*, 47n6, 69, 70
    scientific, 1
    Western, *ix*, 6, 13, 16

denominationalism, 18, 109, 115
discipleship, 7n17, 63, 86, 103
dissonance, cognitive, 32

Name Index

Appial-Kubi, Kofi, *xiv*
Aquinas, Thomas. *See* Thomas
    Aquinas.
Assman, Jan, 52–53
Aulen, Gustaf, 8–9

Barth, Karl, *xiv*, 16, 24, 59, 60, 61, 63,
    65, 82, 90, 99, 113
Berquist, James H., 67
Bevans, Stephen, 29, 30–33, 35, 61,
    61n4, 62,
Boff, Clovodis, 39n38, 58, 96, 96n17
Bonhoeffer, Dietrich, 14n31
Borg, Marcus, 62
Bosch, David, 79
Brown, Robert McAfee, 36

Calvin, John, 11, 89n7, 90, 90n9
Cobb, John, 23
Coe, Shoki, *xiii*, 35, 61, 63, 63n6, 64,
    70, 70n21, 80, 96, 98, 99, 115
Cone, James, *xv*, 64, 64n8
Cruz, Archbishop Oscar, 76

Dawkins, Richard, 4

Eliot, T. S., 50

Foucault, Michel, 16, 19n4, 47, 48,
    48n7, 53, 54n18

Gustafson, James, 40
Gutierrez, Gustavo, 26, 54, 89n7, 92,
    93, 93n14

Habermas, Jürgen, 49, 53
Haight, Roger, 26, 51n14, 104
Hall, Douglas John, *xv*, 64 n.8
Hauerwas, Stanley, *xv*
Hick, John, 23
Hiebert, Paul, 32
Hooft, W. A. Visserít, 13, 22n9, 59
Hume, David, 16

Jenkins, Philip, 18n2, 20, 21, 92n13

Kähler, Martin, 5
Käsemann, Ernest, 39
Kaufman, Gorden, 62
Kelsey, David, 44, 50, 77
Kierkegaard, Søren, 4
Kipling, Rudyard, 2
Knitter, Paul, 23, 62

Lehmann, Paul, *xiii*, 6n14, 35, 38, 42,
    45, 50, 55, 58, 59, 61, 63, 64,
    64n7, 65, 66, 66n14, 73, 74,
    80, 82, 100, 105, 108
Lonergan, Bernard, 41, 108

Marx, Karl, 16, 49
McKinley, President William, 3
Metz, J. B., 26, 27, 27n14, 27n16
Milbank, John, 28n17, 39n38, 65
Minear, Paul, 7, 7n18, 8, 8n19, 9,
    10–11, 11n25
Moltmann, Jürgen, *xv*, 9n20
Mott, John, 1, 1n2, 2

CPSIA information can be obtained at www.ICGtesting.com
Printed in the USA
BVOW080114130712

295068BV00005B/20/P